Genre: Christian literature, Subject: Spiritual Growth,

Words Matter

utterance - the gift of words

Janine Van Tonder
For the love of God and, keeping His words alive.

Words matter.

Copyright © 2024 by Janine van Tonder.

All rights reserved, printed in South Africa. No part of this book may be used or reproduced in any manner whatsoever without written permission, except for brief quotations embodied in critical articles or reviews.

Unless otherwise noted, Scripture quotations are taken from the English Standard Bible Version,

Author Janine van Tonder

Interior design Janine van Tonder

Edited by Janine van Tonder

Co-editor Nadia Bischoff

For information contact:

Words Matter fboek

http://www.website.com

Book and Cover design by Designer

Johnathan Van Tonder from

Relentless Media Productions

ISBN: 978-0-7961-7023-1

First Edition: 2024

The National Library of **South Africa** (NLSA):
Printed in South Africa

1Corinthians 1:5 NKJV
"That you were enriched in everything by Him in all utterance.
and all knowledge…
1Corinthians 1:5 ESV
that in every way you were enriched in Him in all *speech* and all knowledge—

Acknowledgement
To God,
My father
My saviour and the lover of my soul.
For being stubborn with me, strong for me, and never giving up on me.
For always knowing what I needed when I needed it. Your timing is perfect in all things.
For giving me the gift of your love, and the words, with the ability and time to write this book.
I love you!

Acknowledgement
2
To my son Johnathan for always believing in me, you are my heart.

For my spiritual mentor, Pastor Nolan
for always listening when the spirit leads you.
And my spiritual family.
For always being there for us, supporting us, in times of need, and knowing the right words to say at the right time.

Introduction
NOTE FROM THE AUTHOR
Words are like a wildfire when ignited. If words are not used properly, they can set someone's whole life on fire. But if words are used correctly, it can ignite a passion that changes and forms someone's life for the better.

James 3:5 *So also the tongue is a small member, yet it boasts of great things. How great a forest is set ablaze by such a small fire!*

Words can hurt and destroy a soul. You never know when your words are someone's last words before their breaking point. What seeds are you planting with your words today? What kind of fruit will it be? Make sure the words you use today are words you want to eat the fruit of tomorrow.

Proverbs 18:21 *Death and life are in the power of the tongue, and those who love it will eat its fruits.*

Words are a much bigger part of our lives than we realise. We use it all day, every day, but do we ever really realise how big a part, it plays in every part of our lives? It flows into everything we do and affects everything. Our words should be like a fountain of living water, not a wildfire that will destroy.

John 7:38 *Whoever believes in me, as the Scripture has said, 'Out of his heart will flow rivers of living water."*

Proverbs 18:4 *The words of a man's mouth are deep waters; the fountain of wisdom is a bubbling brook.*

Contents

1. Power of words...1
2. Lyrics..11
3. Love unconditional 21
4. Verbal abuse...29
5. Short and sweet 39
6. Not so kind words of advice 47
7. Communication...55
8. Nicknames 63
9. Compliment...75
10. Helper..83
11. Lying 93
12. At your service..101
13. Children 109
14. Shout to the lord...117
15. Build on the rock...125
16. Faith in words..133
17. Answer a call...141
18. Just a joke 151
19. Obedient to God's words............................161
20. Holy Spirit...169
21. A time for words..177
22. Words and unforgiveness...........................185
23. Knowing the truth..193
24. Conclusion..199
    Verse index...203

Proverbs 18:21

Death and life

ARE IN THE POWER

of the **Tongue** and

THOSE WHO LOVE IT WILL EAT ITS FRUITS.

Chapter 1
POWER OF WORDS
John 1:1-2

In the beginning was the Word, and the Word was with God and the Word was God. 2 He was in the beginning with God.

Most of the time we don't even realise we're doing it, putting a smile on someone's face, or a spark back in their heart. Even creating a dream by saying something nice to them. The smallest word can change a heart. Words can inspire, bring joy, and meant a broken heart.

But our words can also damage , kill dreams, and passions. By saying something bitter, destructive, unkind or cruel to someone without even realising that what we are saying is doing damage and leaving marks.

Words Matter

Words can leave lasting scars.

It is unthinkable how a simple word can make someone's day or shatter their spirit. But that is exactly what the problem is! We do not think before we speak.

The words we speak are powerful, so we must start thinking before we speak.

Your mouth can spit venom, or love, mend a broken heart, or break it the choice is yours. Words can even change someone's mind and life when said and articulated correctly.

Choose words of love, comfort, understanding, and compassion, words which create upliftment. It can be very effective when we start thinking before speaking.

It may seem like just words, but the impact they have is enormous. Why do you think that is? Read John 1:1-14, and it gets clear. Think about what you just read. Read the whole chapter of John 1 to make sure it sinks in.

John 1:1-5

In the beginning, was the Word, and the Word was with God, and the Word was God. 2 He was in the beginning with God. 3 All things were made through Him, and without Him was not anything made that was made. 4 In Him was life, and the life was the light of men. 5 The light shines in the darkness, and the darkness has not overcome it.

Words Matter
John 1:14
And the Word became flesh and dwelt among us, and we have seen His glory, glory as of the only Son from the Father, full of grace and truth.

In John 1 we are clearly told that Jesus is the Word who came to us, and the Word was the light. The light that came to live with us. Jesus the Word is the light that came to live with us, came to live in us.

The Word brought forgiveness. The Word brought deliverance, saved our lives, gave us freedom, and joy, and showed us true love, and a new life. The Word came to die on the cross for our sins. Words are powerful look, at what the Word, Jesus, came to do for us.

We need to use our words to do the same for others as the Word did for us. Words make a difference. If Jesus is the Word, how can words not be powerful?

No, we are not God, and our words are not Godly words, but we are the children of God, and therefore, carry power in our words.

John 1:12
But to all who did receive Him, who believed in His name, he gave the right to become children of God.

Galatians 3:26
For in Christ Jesus, you are all sons of God, through faith

Words Matter
Galatians 4:5-7
To redeem those who were under the law, so that we might receive adoption as sons. 6 And because you are sons, God has sent the Spirit of His Son into our hearts, crying, "Abba! Father!" 7 So you are no longer a slave, but a son, and if a son, then an heir through God.

When we become children of God, we become His heirs and inherit His gifts. What does this mean for us? When Jesus commanded us to heal the sick and drive out demons, He also showed us that we are His heirs by giving us His gifts.

What do you think we use to accomplish this command? We use our words. The Holy Spirit guides our words to do it. So, we also inherited His gift for words. The Word came to live with us and gave us His gift of words, so that with it, we can heal the sick, cast out demons, and raise the dead. Including the healing of hearts, souls, and minds.

Matthew 10:8
Heal the sick, raise the dead, cleanse lepers, cast out demons. You received without paying; give without pay.

Mark 16:17-18
And these signs will accompany those who believe in My name, they will cast out demons; they will speak in new tongues; 18 they will pick up serpents with their hands; and if they drink any deadly poison, it will not hurt them; they will lay their hands on the sick, and they will recover."

Words Matter
John 14:12

"Truly, truly, I say to you, whoever believes in me will also do the works that I do; and greater works than these will he do, because I am going to the Father

Jesus is the Word. This has been proven to us by all that He has done through His words; healed the sick, drove away devils, healed hearts, and taught us about love and compassion. He gave us that same gift.

What are you doing with this gift? What do you do with your words? Use it to hurt people, to injure and destroy them, or lift them up closer to God? Words need to be the light used to bring care and value to life. The Word was the light that came to save us. Not an instrument to judge and condemn us to the darkness.

John 12:46-47

I have come into the world as light so that whoever believes in me may not remain in darkness. 47 If anyone hears my words and does not keep them, I do not judge him; for I did not come to judge the world but to save the world.

Are your words building or demolishing? Do you bring light or darkness with your words? Words carry more power than we will ever realise. We all want to be more like Jesus, like the Word of God, so why not start with your words? Words that save, and bring joy, forgiveness, and love.

Words Matter

If we can be perfect when we get our words right, just think what harm we can do if we get our words wrong.

Let the Spirit that lives in you guide you, to use your gift of words, in the right way!

James 3:2-11 Taming the Tongue

For we all stumble in many ways. And if anyone does not stumble in what he says, he is a perfect man, able also to bridle his whole body. 3 If we put bits into the mouths of horses so that they obey us, we guide their whole bodies as well. 4 Look at the ships also: Though they are so large and are driven by strong winds, they are guided by a very small rudder wherever the will of the pilot directs. 5 So also the tongue is a small member, yet it boasts of great things. How great a forest is set ablaze by such a small fire! 6 And the tongue is a fire, a world of unrighteousness. The tongue is set among our members, staining the whole body, setting on fire the entire course of life, and set on fire by hell. 7 For every kind of beast and bird, reptile, and sea creature, can be tamed and has been tamed by mankind, 8 but no human being can tame the tongue. It is a restless evil, full of deadly poison. 9 With it we bless our Lord and Father, and with it, we curse people who are made in the likeness of God. 10 From the same mouth come blessing and cursing. My brothers, these things ought not to be so. *11 Does a spring pour forth from the same opening both fresh and saltwater?*

Words Matter
1 John 5:7 KJV

For there are three that bear record in heaven, the Father, the Word, and the Holy Ghost: and these three are one.

What are the key takeaways from this chapter?

1. Power of words.
2. Words can change hearts and lives.
3. Start thinking before speaking.
4. Jesus is the Word.
5. As God's children, our words carry power.
6. We inherited His Gift of words.
7. The Word is the light, what are you doing with your words?
8. If we are perfect when we get our words right, how much damage can wrong words do
9. 1 John 2:6 whoever says he abides in him ought to walk in the same way in which he walked.

Notes

Ephesians 5:18-20

And do not get drunk with wine, for that is debauchery, but be
filled with the Spirit,
19 Addressing one another in Psalms and Hymns and spiritual songs, singing and making melody **to the Lord** with your heart,

20 ***Giving thanks always*** AND FOR EVERYTHING TO GOD THE FATHER IN THE NAME OF OUR LORD JESUS CHRIST.

Chapter 2
LYRICS

Psalms 96:1

Oh, sing to the LORD a new song. sing to the LORD, all the earth!

Music = words with passion. Music has a path straight to our hearts and soul. The Words in songs connect our thoughts and our hearts. It is a universal language, which we all understand. Music evokes strong emotions that resonate with our hearts. It can make us sad, happy, angry, and calm. It brings back experiences good and bad and makes us nostalgic for times gone by. It touches us in our deepest soul. It makes us feel understood and connected. Certain emotions are just better described in lyrics! Praise and worship are one of them. That is why music is one of God's treasured and beloved

Words Matter

forms of worship. It opens our hearts and souls to Him.

Just like in other places, words carry a lot of power in music, but more so because we will sing without thinking what we are singing. Simply because the beat or melody draws us in, not realising that the words start to live in us.

One of the greatest ways of giving our mind, heart, thanks, love, and submission to God is to bring our words of praise to Him in songs.

Psalms 9:1-2

A Psalm of David. I will give thanks to the LORD with my whole heart; I will recount all of Your wonderful deeds.2 I will be glad and exult in You; I will sing praise to Your name, O Most High.

Right through the Bible, God's people sang to Him. Maria had a special song for God in Luke 1:46, Hanna in 1 Samuel 2:1, Zachariah in Luke 1:67 as well as King David in 2 Samuel 22:1. God's people have always loved to sing for Him.

Praise and worship connect us to God. It helps us be closer to Him and allows us to express our love for Him. It is a grand form of prayer, to lift our words of worship to God through song.

But then lyrics also go wrong and are used to poison. The enemy has taken this wonderful gift that God gave us and twisted it and turned it for bad also. When listening carefully to more and more of the words, in so many of our music genres, it gets scary when realising what is being said in so many songs.

Words Matter
James 3:8-11

But no human being can tame the tongue. It is a restless evil, full of deadly poison. 9 With it, we bless our Lord and Father, and with it, we curse people who are made in the likeness of God. 10 From the same mouth come blessing and cursing. *My brothers, these things ought not to be so. 11 Does a spring pour forth from the same opening both fresh and saltwater?*

"It's not just in secular music—this subtle distortion is infiltrating Christian music as well. A single poorly used word can sow seeds of uncertainty in our hearts. One misplaced phrase can shift a song from genuine worship to something that dishonours God and casts doubt on His unshakable love for us. Words matter deeply, even in the songs we sing to praise Him."

You must listen to the words you sing, not just sing along. Realise what the words that you are singing mean. Let the meaning of the words in the song resonate with you, and then it will carry more value, or you will realise that it is not right to sing or say it at all.

Think about this for a moment!

Listening and singing along to a song over and over is like chanting over and over. So, to whom are you chanting, and what are you chanting?

What are the words of the song you are singing over and over? Life and death are in the power of the tongue so what are you singing, and saying? What are the words you are giving life to in your soul?

Words Matter

Are you worshipping God, something else, or someone else? Are you submitting to God in song or to the things of the world? Do you believe in the words you are singing?

"Holy Ground"
(Chorus)
This is holy ground, Lord, holy ground, Lord, holy ground.
This is holy ground, Lord, holy ground, Lord, holy ground.
(Verse 1)
Lead us in Your way Lord, in Your way, in Your way.
Lead us in Your way Lord, in Your way, in Your way.
(Verse 2)
Show us to Your heart, Lord, to Your heart, to Your heart.
Show us to Your heart, Lord, to Your heart, to Your heart.
(Pre-Chorus)
We bow before You, we lift Your name,
Standing in wonder, we won't be the same.
Heaven is moving, Your presence is near,
Here in this moment, we have no fear.
(Chorus – Repeat)
This is holy ground, Lord, holy ground, Lord, holy ground.
This is holy ground, Lord, holy ground, Lord, holy ground.
(Verse 3)

Words Matter

This is how You work, Lord, how You work, Lord, in our lives.
This is how You work, Lord, how You work, Lord, in our lives.
(Bridge)
Let Your fire fall, let Your glory reign,
Purify our hearts, we won't be the same.
Chains are breaking, the lost are found,
As we stand here on holy ground.

Are the words of the song you are singing bringing honour and glory to God, or not? What are you singing? What are you saying? Worshipping God with words only, is senseless if your heart is not in it, filled with love for Him. If you do not even realise what you are singing, it has no meaning to Him!

1Corinthians 13:1

If I speak in the tongues of men and of angels but have not love, I am a noisy gong or a clanging cymbal.

We should listen to the right music for many reasons,' but to name just one. The wrong words, in the wrong music, will get stuck in our heads and become a part of our lives, we will give life to it. How then will we be able to serve God with our lips and hearts in song if the things of the world are still stuck in our minds? Music should bring us closer to God, not separate us from His love.

Matthew 15:7-9

You hypocrites! Well, did Isaiah prophesy of you, when he said: 8 "This people Honors. me with their lips, but their heart is far from me, 9 in vain do they worship me, teaching as doctrines the commandments of men."

Words Matter

Worship is love. The more we understand love, the more we will understand worship, and the better and greater our worship to God will be. The understanding of worship is the understanding of love. God wants us to worship Him fully and completely and, in that worship, we will come to understand His love. Love so great that we will not want to do anything but worship God. If we can understand love, we can also understand worshipping God. So, if we surrender in worship, we can surrender in love to Him.

Remember when we worship, we lay it all down. The burdens, the worries, the fears we have found. Lifting our hands, we offer it all, surrendering all.

When your minds begin to stray in worship, and the worldly things try pulling us away, stopping us from fully letting go. Just fix your eyes; lift your voice. Choose to trust, make the choice. Receive his peace.

Keep worshipping, keep lifting high. Let His presence fill your life. The battle has already been won, the victory's done, what the enemy meant for pain, God is turning it for grace.

As we worship, our desire to focus on God is stronger than the flesh, enabling us to worship with greater devotion and release the things of the flesh more quickly.

So, keep giving, keep letting go, feel His healing overflow.

Words Matter

Allowing your worship to become purer, keeping your hands lifted high, heart open wide, giving to God, and letting go.

Know what you are singing, so your words in your worship can carry you high to him.

Psalms 100:1-2

Make a joyful noise to the LORD, all the earth! 2 Serve the LORD with gladness! Come into His presence with singing!

What are the key takeaways from this chapter?

1. Lyrics
2. Music evokes strong emotions in us, that connect us all.
3. A good way to give everything to God is in worship.
4. God's people have been doing it throughout the ages.
5. The enemy uses lyrics in music to let your words go wrong.
6. Bad words permeate all genres of music.
7. Know and listen to the words you are singing.
8. Who do you submit to in song?
9. Do you believe what you are singing, and will it honour God?
10. Worship is love.
11. Love is worship.
12. Your words and heart should speak together when you worship in song

1 Corinthians 13:4-7

LOVE IS PATIENT AND KIND

love does not envy or boast

It is not arrogant ₅or rude.

It does not insist on its own way

it is not irritable or resentful.

₆ It does not rejoice at wrongdoing

But rejoices with the truth.

₇ Love bears all things, believes all things, hopes all things, endures all things.

Chapter 3
LOVE UNCONDITIONAL
John 15:13-15

Greater love has no one than this to lay down his life for one's friends 14 *You are my friends if you do what I command you.* 15 *No longer do I call you servants, for the servant does not know what his master is doing, but I have called you friends, for all that I have heard from My Father I have made known to you.*

God's love for us is unconditional, so we must also give unconditional love. No greater love is there than, the love God shows us daily. God gave us the perfect example of how to love completely and with everything we have. As a reminder, He left us the holy communion so that we will always be

Words Matter

able to remember His undying love for us. Do you still remember His love, when you are participating in the Holy Communion? Do you still honour that undying Love, with your words, to others?

Love, the word that makes the world go round. Even though the word is small there is nothing small about the power that the word love carries. Love is the most precious possession we will ever have and must be preserved at all costs. That's why it is so wrong when love, is used as nothing more than a word.

1 John 3:18 NIV
Dear children, let us not love with words or speech. But with actions and in truth.

Love is one of the most important things in our lives, without it, we are a clanging cymbal. Yet it is the most misused word in all of time.

Whether it is out of ignorance because we cannot fully understand what love is, or whether it is done for a deceitful reason. The word love is often misused, or not used at all when it should be used, or for all the wrong reasons.

One thing that should never happen is that the words "I love you" go unheard because they were never said, out of fear or pride, but the words should never be empty.

When the different levels of love are understood and used correctly, we will use it better and feel more comfortable doing so.

Words Matter

AGAPE - Unconditional, Sacrificial Love
Agape is God's perfect, selfless, and unconditional love. It is the highest form of love. Love that gives without expecting anything in return.

EROS - Romantic, Passionate Love
Eros is romantic love between a husband and wife.

STORGE - Family, Parental Love.
Storge is natural affection and love found within families-parents for children, siblings for each other. It reflects loyalty and care.

PHILIA - Friendship, Brotherly Love.
Philia is affectionate love between close friends and fellow believers. It's built on shared experiences, mutual respect, and deep connection.

With these three little words, "I love you," we can change lives and hearts. Even if we don't use them when we are supposed to, it leaves a mark, good or bad. Listen to your heart and let God guide your words.

We must love everyone and say it to them often. Just make sure you say it, and they understand it in the right context, or it may cause harm rather than the love you intended. Love carries a lot of power over good and evil, especially when we use it in the will of God. Unfortunately, people like to use the word love for their gain, so that they can use people like puppets. You must let the Holy Spirit guide you when to use the words "I love you" and when to receive it. The actions and words must align.

Unfortunately, the world has deformed love so much that we cannot see, understand or even feel real love

Words Matter

without God, not that we should do anything without God but we need to look at Him to feel it more clearly. Love is the greatest commandment that God gave us. So, do you not think He takes it seriously? Don't you think there will be consequences if you use it wrongly and for the wrong reasons? Yes, we must love everybody, but with a love that builds up and does not tear down. When it tears down, it is not love.

Unfortunately, it's being used so casually, and for all the wrong reasons, as if it were a game that is being played, and not as God intended it to. Love is not a game; it's God's greatest gift to us, and the actions must follow the words.

The more love you give, the more you will receive. Love makes the world go round, love for God, our fellow man, our country, work, nature and love for our culture. If we start giving love unconditionally and not to get, but to give only, then we will understand God's love more clearly.

We must love fully and completely, not only in words but in heart and deed. Distinguishing clearly between the different types of love in our lives.

Love is not just a word, but an action, making it impossible for us to hide how we feel. You can see love and feel love, not just hear it. Therefore, let your love be unconditional, and your actions will match your words.

Matthew 22:37-39 NIV

Jesus replied: "'Love the Lord your God with all your heart and with all your soul and with all your mind.' This is the first and greatest commandment. 39 And the second is like it: 'Love your neighbour as yourself.'

Words Matter
John 3:16
"For God so loved the world, that he gave his only son, that whoever believes in Him should not perish but have eternal life...

1 Corinthians 13:13
So now faith, hope, and love abide, these three; but the greatest of these is love.

What are the key takeaways from this chapter?

1. Love unconditionally!
2. Give unconditional love because God gives us His love unconditionally.
3. Love is not just a word.
4. Love is one of the most misused words.
5. There are different types of love.
6. Even if it is not said, it can harm.
7. Let God guide your words of love.
8. Make sure your love is understood correctly.
9. The word love is misused; all the time let the Holy Spirit guide you.
10. There is repercussions if you take advantage of love.
11. Love not only in words but in deeds.
12. Unconditional love is laying down your life as Jesus did for us.
13. Rom 12:9 Let love be genuine. Abhor what is evil; hold fast to what is good. 10 Love one another with brotherly affection. Outdo one another in showing honor.

---Psalms 141:3---

Set a guard over my mouth

LORD

Keep watch over the door of

my lips.

Chapter 4
VERBAL ABUSE
James 1:19
Know this, my beloved brothers: let every person be quick to hear, slow to speak, slow to anger.

The spoken word is one of the most powerful things in this world. It breaks my heart to hear how people waste their words and use such a wonderful gift that God gave them to do harm.

Yes, **sticks and stones** will **break my bones**, but words can and will do harm. They will do so much worse: they can, and will, break your heart and destroy your soul. Because words is indeed mightier than the sword.

Words Matter
Ephesians 6:13
Therefore, take up the whole armour of God, that you may be able to withstand in the evil day, and having done all, to stand firm.

No matter how strong you think you are, the power of words is so much stronger. Only if you are rooted in God, and you are wearing the full armour of God, are you protected.

Do you even realise all the self-esteem you have lost over the years, all your insecurities and self-doubt are mostly due to the wounding of spiteful words people have spoken to you over the years. Chipping away at us over time, bit by bit.

So bad that we even started using our words against ourselves, to chip away at what was left of our self-esteem. We get so used to being put down by others, that we start to self-abuse.

Every time you tell yourself you are not good enough for something or someone, for that job or promotion you want, or when you look in the mirror, and think "I have terrible hair", or "I have too many freckles", "my nose is too flat", "or my eyes are too big", "my hair is too curly". Not only are you using your words to tear yourself down, but you are also insulting God's design.

STOP IT! You are a part of God's perfect creation.

Instead of using our words to thank God for all that we have. Eyes that see, ears to hear, a mouth

Words Matter

to smile with, we use our words to tear ourselves down. Even if the words are only in our minds, they still do a lot of damage. The words that other people have used so many times to tear us down, we have now started using, to tear ourselves apart. And it's not as if extra help is needed, the world is already doing enough damage with their, insults, lies, dishonesty, hypocrisy and greed, anger, hatred, and jealousy

Colossians 3:8
But now you must put them all away anger, wrath, malice, slander and obscene talk from your mouth.

Verbal abusers have become so good at inserting words of destruction everywhere in our lives. We don't even notice anymore when they do it. They make it sound like it's something good when they insult you.

A lot of verbal abusers don't even know they are an abuser. All they want to do is voice how they feel inside on to others and their words are always negative, bad, and off-putting.

Putting negative thoughts on someone else makes them feel less alone. Simply making someone else feel the way they feel is not wrong for them; it is normal.

They do not know or understand happiness.

Verbal abusers are always starting arguments, using their words to manipulate people into a fight. Then, pretending to be the victim to justify

Words Matter

their behaviour and actions and they just love to add "It's just a joke."

The result of being abused over and over by someone's bad words is silence. The victims start to believe that, not only are they not worthy enough to speak up or do anything about it, but they simply keep quiet because they want to try and avoid another fight that will make them feel that they are not good enough. This is exactly what the abuser wants so that they can keep on walking all over the abused.

Pray to protect your heart, soul, and mind from these types of people, and never get silent when someone throws negative words at you. Talk to someone about it, and if it's a relationship you feel you want to preserve, talk to that person about it and try to save the relationship without continuing to live with the verbal abuse. But never get quiet and keep everything inside. Your words are important to be heard.

Be alert when you start to get quiet for no good reason. It is usually a sign that you are a victim of verbal abuse, because you are afraid to speak up. You can only protect your heart from this if you are aware that it is happening. Most of the time, we don't even realise it.

Proverbs 4:23-24

Keep your heart with all vigilance, for from it flow the springs of life. 24 Put away from you crooked speech and put devious talk far from you.

Words Matter

Verbal abuse is everywhere, and like a thief in the night, we don't see it coming. Pray that your spiritual ears will be open to these people and that you will hear when they want to do harm.

Have you ever been in a conversation where someone says something bad about another person? Little do they know it's something true about you too; they are also insulting you and do not even know it.

All some people want to do is say something bad about someone even if there is no good reason for it. Just because they do not like it or understand something, they use their words to knock it off, not caring who hears it or who gets hurt by their words.

Verbal abuse takes many forms. One of them gossiping. Even if the person being gossiped about never finds out about it, which is unlikely, harm is being done. The person or persons who heard it will now also become self-aware and always try not to become the reason for the next gossip on the same subject.

James 4:11

Do not speak evil against one another, brothers. The one who speaks against a brother or judges his brother, speaks evil against the law and judges the law. But if you judge the law, you are not a doer of the law but a judge.

Words Matter

This is another good reason why we should always use our words for good, and not talk about other people behind their backs.

Always use good words that are uplifting whether you are talking to, or about someone else. Use only words, which bear good fruit. Whether the person for whom the words are intended hears it or not.

Without realising it, we can do harm with our words to body, soul, and spirit.

Simply because we feel different about something or want to make a joke off it, are tired or irritated, or are having a bad day. Saying something because we can, does not make it right. Always think before you speak!

It is important to learn not to accept other people's bad words about us and over our lives. Ask God to help you to forgive and forget.

Verbal abusers come in all shapes and sizes male, female, rich or poor, strong and weak. And even the victims come from all walks of life.

Ephesians 4:29
Let no corrupting talk come out of your mouths, but only such as is good for building up, as fits the occasion, that it may give grace to those who hear.

Proverbs 12:25
Anxiety in a man's heart weighs him down, but a good word makes him glad.

Words Matter

What are the key takeaways from this chapter?

1. Verbal abuse.
2. Yes, sticks and stones will break my bones, but words can and will harm.
3. Only by being rooted in God will you be saved from negative words.
4. Spiteful words damage our self-esteem.
5. Stop the self-abuse.
6. We don't even realise we are being abused.
7. Pray to protect your heart, soul, and mind from abusers.
8. Verbal abusers are everywhere, and we don't see it coming.
9. Verbal abusers will insult you without even knowing it.
10. Verbal abuse takes many forms.
11. We can harm with our words. Because we feel different about some things.
12. Verbal abusers come in all shapes and sizes.
13. Pro 3:33 The LORD's curse is on the house of the wicked, but he blesses the dwelling of the righteous.

Notes

Proverbs 15:23 ASV

A man hath joy by the answer of his mouth

And a Word

spoken in due season,

HOW GOOD IS IT?

Chapter 5
SHORT AND SWEET
Matthaeus 4:19
And he said to them, "Follow me, and I will make you fishers of men."

Jesus said follow me! and changed the lives of many. Short and sweet can be powerful when used at the right time, right place, and in the right way. Making a short and clear statement can be reassuring. It shows confidence in what you are saying and doing. Fewer words can be more when needed. But there is a fine line between short and sweet and not saying enough. I am not talking about speaking up for yourself. That is a chapter on its own. What I'm talking about is not using enough words or too many words. Saying too much about something can make you seem

Words Matter

insecure, unsure, and even false, about what you say. Not saying enough can make the meaning of your words unclear.

For example, saying "no", you have the right to say "no". You don't always have to explain yourself. Sometimes you just know it's a "no" and find it hard to say the words to explain why. You just know it's a "no". Have you ever thought it's the Holy Spirit, who guides you to say "no", (that little voice that talks to you)? That is why you cannot find the words to explain why it is "no".

But saying "no" brings out a strong reaction in most people. So, remember just saying "no", with no reason to the wrong person, can damage or hurt them in more ways than one. Sometimes just saying "no" is important and can be powerful, but you need to learn when.

Adding something small to your "no" can make a big difference. Make it feel less cold. "No, I'm unable to". "No, not possible". "No, that's not working for me". "No, not at this time". "No, I'm not currently prepared for that". No, I am uncomfortable with that."

There is a time and place for everything. Let the spirit guide you on when to keep it short and when to say more. It's ok to just say "no" but never lie to give a reason for your "no". Leave it at a short and sweet NO rather than tell a lie as a reason. Short and sweet does not always mean you will get something done faster! Short and sweet have

Words Matter

advantages but speaking briefly and quickly is not the same thing as short and sweet.

Not using enough words, leaving things out when you speak, or when you are in a rush, or not in the mood. Is not saving time! Don't assume people know what you're thinking about when you don't make yourself clear.

Everyone's point of view is different. God made us all unique, which makes us all see things differently. Communicating properly is key.

People will misunderstand what you say, and what you want them to know and do. You can't get angry with them when you don't speak correctly or clearly. Not everyone can read between the lines. Speak up and in proper sentences.

The world has become such a rush that people not only don't think before they speak, but also started shortening everything when talking. Always doing everything in a rush!

Remember, not only can people not read your mind, but their way of thinking is different from yours. Make proper sentences when you speak, don't always make everything short and powerful. It can do harm. This does not mean speaking to them as if they are children, it simply means speaking clearly.

Those shortened words and sentences are passed on from one person to the next, and the message is mistranslated again and again. Your intentions are misunderstood because you wanted to speak

Words Matter

too quickly and briefly. We must use words and sentences correctly and not in contractions.

The same counts for when we want to get a "quick" word in. We often want to quickly give our opinion on something and be able to get a word into the conversation, but that doesn't mean you must use fewer words, besides, then you won't get the right message out and you will be misunderstood.

Speak up! Especially when giving God's message. Never rush God's words and message. People will misunderstand you. When we convey God's Word, we must make sure we use the right words about the Word of God.

When there is a passion in you for God's Word, you will always want to share the message of God, when necessary, but messing it up is not the way. Stop rumbling your words off, speak properly so that people can understand you clearly.

Short and sweet is not so short and sweet if it ends in a misunderstanding. Less can be more but has a time and place. More is important. There's a time and place for all things.

The same goes for short and sweet. Sometimes it is all that is needed, but some things need to be made clear. Learn the difference. Less is more but more can be less.

Remember, this is not the same as someone who always needs to have their opinion said and

Words Matter

always has something to say to cover their actions or bad intentions with their words.

Proverbs 17:27-28

Whoever restrains his words Has knowledge, and he who has a cool spirit is a man of understanding. 28 Even a fool who keeps silent is considered wise, when he closes his lips, he is deemed intelligent.

What are the key takeaways from this chapter?

1. Short and sweet.
2. Short and sweet can be powerful.
3. Less words can be more.
4. There is a fine line between being brief and to the point and not explaining yourself.
5. Is it okay to just say no?
6. Speaking briefly and quickly is different from short and sweet.
7. You can't get angry when you don't speak correctly or clearly.
8. Stop rushing your words.
9. Shortened sentences can lead to big misunderstandings.
10. Never rush God's message. Make sure you use the correct words.
11. Pro 10:18 The one who conceals hatred has lying lips, and whoever utters slander is a fool. 19 When words are many, transgression is not lacking, but whoever restrains his lips is prudent.

Matthew 12:36-37

I TELL YOU, ON THE DAY OF JUDGMENT
PEOPLE WILL GIVE ACCOUNT FOR EVERY
careless word they speak,

37 For by your Words, you will be justified, and by your Words, you **will be condemned.**

Chapter 6
NOT SO KIND WORDS OF ADVICE
Ephesians 4:29
Let no corrupting talk come out of your mouths, but only such as is good for building up, as fits the occasion, that it may give grace to those who hear.

Not so kind words of advice. It's always good and refreshing to get advice from someone when you must make a decision, you're unsure about. But who you ask makes a difference to the type of advice you will receive. It is always a good idea to talk to someone who knows you and will better understand the point of view you are speaking from. God is of course the best counsellor because he knows us best, if we can only remember to go to

Words Matter

him first for advice. The same also applies when you give advice.

Ask, have you prayed about it? Before you start giving advice. Have you ever considered that the words of advice you give someone might not be a clever idea? Advising because you see or think something in someone's life is wrong or does not look acceptable to you is not kind. Especially if it was not asked for.

Consider this. We are so quick to judge other people that we think we also know what is better for them. We see or hear something, and think we know better, and do not consider that the words of advice we give them can do harm and hurt them even more, making them feel judged.

Consider the consequences of your words. Just because it seems not right in your life doesn't mean it is not right for their life. Make sure they want and need your advice. You need to know the whole story before you start giving advice.

James 1:19
Know this, my beloved brothers: let every person be quick to hear, slow to speak, slow to anger.

Think about it very carefully before you give advice not asked for. Are you sure you know the person well enough to give advice? Do you know why they did or said what they did, or made the decision they did? Make sure you have your facts straight and think of their needs before you give them advice. You may do harm rather than good.

Words Matter

Your words may not come out so kindly! You may seem judgmental and unfriendly!

Your friendly words of advice may just make a difficult decision even worse. Get the facts in front of you before you give your opinion.

Your words may be the last strain that someone can deal with in an already difficult decision they need to make. Advise according to their needs, not your opinion. Your words might not be as friendly as you think!

Ask God to show you what advice they need. Let Him guide your lips, let the Holy Spirit guide you. Leave your opinion out of it and make sure they want and need your help. They may only need you to listen, to have understanding and not to give advice.

But most of all, do not just go around handing out your advice, thinking you are being friendly, especially if it was not asked for! We all want to help someone in need, even if it is just to talk to them and give words of comfort.

But do you know as much as you think you do? Remember, everyone's point of view is different. You may be missing important info. Do you have all the facts?

If you feel someone is in real need of help. Rather, ask someone with experience to help.

Unsolicited advice can make someone feel ashamed or not good enough, the wrong words will only do more harm.

Words Matter
Proverbs 12:5-6

The thoughts of the righteous are just; the counsels of the wicked are deceitful. 6 The words of the wicked lie in wait for blood, but the mouth of the upright delivers them.

What are the key takeaways from this chapter?

1. Not-so-kind words of advice.
2. Where do you go to get advice?
3. God knows us best.
4. Was the advice asked for?
5. Words of advice can harm.
6. Know the story before advising.
7. Make sure you have your facts straight
8. Leave your opinion out of it.
9. Ask God to show you what is needed.
10. Ask someone with experience to help.
11. Wrong words will only do more harm than good.

Notes

Notes

{ James 3:5-6 }

So also, the tongue is a small member,

--Yet it boasts of great things.--

How great a forest is set ablaze

By such a small fire!

6 And the tongue is a fire,

A world of unrighteousness.

The Tongue

is set among our members, staining the whole body,

setting on fire the entire course of life,

and set on fire by hell.

Chapter 7
Communication

1 Corinthians 1:5-7

That in every way you were enriched in Him in all speech and all knowledge 6 even as the testimony about Christ was confirmed among you. 7 so that you are not lacking in any gift, as you wait for the revealing of our Lord Jesus Christ.

Communication is one of the most important things we as humans must do. There are so many amazing ways to do it today, but it has just become a way to communicate less.

The fact that you no longer need to look someone in the eye to talk or communicate with them does not mean that you no longer bear responsibility for your words and actions.

Words Matter

Communication is a gift and a responsibility that needs to be handled correctly.

God's message in Proverbs 18:20 still stands. You will be held accountable for every word, for every wildfire you ignited with your words. Whether you call, sms, DM, pm, email, use a letter, or your lips do the talking. The actions of those words are your responsibility.

So, stop thinking that when doing things faster, you can fall short in your words and be rude when communicating. No matter how you are going to communicate. Still do it with respect and love towards your neighbours.

Mattheus 22:37-39

And he said to him, "You shall love the Lord your God with all your heart and with all your soul and with all your mind. 38 This is the great and first commandment. 39 And a second is like it. You shall love your neighbour as yourself.

Start talking to each other, talk to strangers, with your customers, a neighbour, even your landlord. You will be amazed at who and what you discover in the people around you when you communicate more. I mean talk, really talk, not just "hi hello", "how are you?" Connect with someone! There are amazing children of God all around us that we don't even know or see.

Their words may just speak to you, a message, an answer that you have been waiting for. You may just find that you are not as alone in your matters

Words Matter

as you thought. God sends wonderful people on our path in life. If we can only learn to properly communicate.

You may just learn something new to honour and thank God for. You may just be the one whom God has sent on that person's path to help them or to lead them back to God. One word can make a difference.

If we can only learn to use our gift of words, to communicate with people, to get to know them and show them our hearts and learn their hearts. Then we can be better disciples. How can we be disciples of God if we don't even know how to use our words anymore?

As God's disciples, we also need to connect properly to God so that we can communicate His message better to His children. With all the amazing ways He has given us to do it, we need to remember to do it correctly and properly.

Communication is the key to the heart of God's children. If we cannot learn to use our words to communicate our feelings and hearts, how can we hear the feelings in the words of God's children?

We need to learn how to hear and feel words to communicate better.

You should feel the words when you speak and listen to others instead of disconnecting from communication, no matter how we connect.

Proverbs 27:17
Iron sharpens iron and one man sharpens another.

Words Matter

What are the key takeaways from this chapter?

1. Communication.
2. Communication is a responsibility that needs to be handled correctly.
3. Do you feel the words when you listen to others?
4. Bad communication can lead to a wildfire of words.
5. All types of communication fall under the Proverbs 18v 21 rule.
6. Really connect to people.
7. God sends people our way for a reason.
8. Use your gift of words to connect.
9. If we cannot use our words anymore, how can we hear the words of God's children?

Notes

Notes

Isaiah

43:1

But now thus says the LORD,
He who created you,
O Jacob, He who formed you, O Israel
"Fear not, for I have redeemed you;
I have called you by name,
you are mine."

Chapter 8
Nicknames

Ecclesiastes 7:1
A good name is better than precious ointment, and the day of death than the day of birth.

There is power in a name. Just watch someone you have not known long react when you refer to them by name. Acknowledging that you know who they are means something. A name carries power. It forms a part of who we are, a part of our identity. Therefore, the enemy always wants to harm it. One way is by using us to give others nicknames and thereby labelling them.
Nicknames, the spectrum on it is so big and does so much damage, to people of all ages. The damage that can be done is so bad that only God's, hand in your life will help repair this damage.

Words Matter

Labelling someone is never right. It is done everywhere and touches all ages. It starts when we are born, right up to a grey old age. People do it with their children, friends, wives, husbands, and even colleagues. Trying to define them by giving them a nickname which is not always good and are not acceptable.

People like to put labels on others, giving them all kinds of nicknames like Stick, Stinky, Prins, bunny, tiger, champ, tower, rebel, trouble, slick, shorty, doll, and my Angel. Some of them are good and others not so good, but whether it's a good nickname or a bad nickname it influences the person who receives it. It starts to become a part of their identity.

Fortunately, most nicknames do not stick. This is good because no one should be identified because of someone else's opinion about them, or because of a certain time or circumstance in their life. Only you and God can define our identity.

Whether it's a good or a bad nickname that you give to someone, the nickname forms and creates people's opinions about that person which can give people the wrong impression about someone. I'm not trying to say that we should never give nicknames. Just be careful, very careful in the words you choose to create someone's identity.

Do you really want that type of responsibility or influence in helping to make and create someone's personality?

Words Matter

A nickname can also be so beautiful, affectionate, and special. To be called something special and nice by someone who knows and notices you, in your deepest, deep centre, is very special, but you should never let it change who you are and affect your personality.

Romans 12:2

Do not be conformed to this world, but be transformed by the renewal of your mind, that by testing you may discern what is the will of God, what is good and acceptable and perfect.

It can be so nice and beautiful when someone calls you "my love" or "angel," but there is also the right time and place for it and doing it so much that it looks like you have forgotten that person's real name is also not right and makes it less special. More is not always better when it comes to this.

Don't give someone negative words for nicknames like momster, stinky or rebel. It's not nice to be called something negative even if you think it's a cute or endearing nickname.

Both of you may think it doesn't matter, but in the long run, it influences us all. It's a seed that gets planted in the back of the mind and comes to the front when you least expect it.

Negative words as nicknames are just someone putting a bad label on you. The sad part is most of the time they don't even realise they are doing it.

Words Matter

You do not have to accept it. Speak up and make them remember your name, and use your name. Bad nicknames are just another form of bullying.

So, they don't want to bother to learn your name, or they want to belittle you.

They will rather give you a bad nickname, which of course will also help them feel better about themselves, if they can break you're spirit down a bit with it (most likely because someone broke them with a nickname). It's a simple act of not caring and considering someone else's feelings.

It is important to know and remember that all these nicknames that make you feel bad about yourself, ultimately, have nothing to do with you but are the result of someone else's self-esteem and problems that they need to sort out.

It's a vicious cycle which keeps going on and on if we don't stop it. Fortunately, we have the Holy Spirit that protects us against such things as bad nicknames and from other people's bad self-esteem latching on to us because of a bad nickname. Unfortunately, sometimes we realise it too late because we don't listen to that little voice of the Holy Spirit that wants to protect us.

Here is the thing!

Some nicknames are harmless and loving, but how Sure are you?

You might mean it lovingly, but how do you know that there is not something in that person's life or past that makes it not good?

Words Matter

There may have been someone abusive that called them that, or someone they have lost, and you keep on reminding them of it. Maybe someone used that nickname to belittle them.

To give someone a nickname, you must know them very well if you do not want to do damage. So, stick with a name that will lift someone up and make them feel better about themselves, and not break them down. Better still, stick with the name their mama gave them, real names.

It also makes a difference to whom you give the nickname and from whom it is received. Giving someone else's husband or wife a sweet nickname, for instance, will not be acceptable. Just think of the consequences of that!!

Then there are the unknown nicknames. It can be such a dangerous thing to call people nicknames that you heard others have called them, since you don't know where the nicknames came from.

The person may just think you are doing it for the same reason as the other person. It will make them think that if more than one calls me that, then it must be true.

The same goes for diminutive names that people like to use to belittle someone. Isn't it amazing how loved we can feel when someone uses a diminutive name for us like "lovely", "sweetie, "or "honey" but unfortunately, it is more often used to belittle and tear people down, rather than out of love.

Words Matter

I heard a conversation between two colleagues one morning, and the guy who is known for his bad attitude and back-talking to everyone, greeted the other man using his name more than once in a diminutive form. Then he used other words in diminutive forms while speaking to him as if he were a baby.

After the conversation was over, I took the opportunity to talk to the man and I asked him if he was aware of what the other one was trying to do, talking to him like that. This guy, on the other hand, someone who always tries to avoid conflict, gave me a simple but shocking answer.

"Oh, I know, but do you know you do it too? Use diminutive names." The words shocked me, and I realised. That even though I thought I was doing it from a loving side of respect, because the men I was doing it with were older than me and had been working at the company longer than me.

I suddenly realised that they might not see it that way and that in the end it can be seen as nothing but disrespectful.

Everyone is made so unique by God's hands that we cannot treat everyone the same. Our words and actions have an impact on people's lives, and it is time we realised this.

It's better to treat everyone right from the start, and with love, than you can't get it wrong.

The next question is, of course, what's the right way and what is the wrong way? The answer it's

Words Matter

simple. Listen to the holy spirit and read your Bible every day, and you will grow, grow, grow. It's all there, laid down in the Word of God. The more you read the Bible, the more you will know right from wrong.

You simply have to start.

The Name that is above all names will hold you accountable for the nicknames you give out to others. Whether it's because you want to tear someone's name down or build it up. You bear the weight of the damage you do!

Proverbs 11:9

With his mouth, the godless man would destroy his neighbour, but by knowledge, the righteous are delivered.

What were the key takeaways from this chapter?

1. Nicknames.
2. A name carries power.
3. Giving someone a nickname is like giving them a label.
4. It is being done to everyone, everywhere.
5. Good or bad a nickname influences a person.
6. Only God should have an impact on our identity.
7. Don't let a nickname change your personality.
8. Bad nicknames are just another form of bullying.
9. Stick to real names; it is safer.

Words Matter

10. Stay away from unknown nicknames and diminutive nicknames.
11. You simply have to start.
12. Everyone is made so unique by God's hands, that's why we cannot treat everyone the same.

Notes

Notes

Job 4:4

Your *words have* upheld *him* who *was* stumbling, *and* you *have* made firm *the* feeble *knees.*

Chapter 9
Compliment
Ephesians 4:29
Let no corrupting talk come out of your mouths, but only such as is good for building up, as fits the occasion, that it may give grace to those who hear.

When we use our words to compliment people we enrich life's whether it's about something big or small. The seed we plant with our words can grow to become beautiful and virtuous. It can strengthen and repair poor self-esteem and a weak soul. Our words can bear fruit of joy.

Have you ever seen that smile on someone's face when you compliment them whether it's inward or outward, or about what they've done or how they look? If you see something that you feel is worthy of a compliment, give it. Don't just let it be, it can make a difference in someone's life.

Words Matter

Now, think what it can mean to someone, if you can turn that smile inward. If you can not only touch someone's heart, but their soul with your words and compliments. You can help repair a cracked self-esteem with your words.

Take for example "please" and "thank you," such small words but they carry so much power. Most of us don't even realise that "please" and "thank you" are compliments.

"Thank you" means I am happy and satisfied with what you have done. COMPLIMENT

"Please," says I know you will be good at this; can you help me with it? COMPLIMENT

(It's important to remember that even if people don't use it when they talk to you, it doesn't mean you don't deserve it. Most people just don't realise they need to say "please" and "thank you.")

Just saying "thank you" when someone has done something can make such a difference. More so if you can elaborate on "thank you," or "please." Personalising it is so much better.

"Thank you, I appreciate it" or "Thank you for your **kind** words. It means a lot to me". "Thank **you** for **your** prayers". "Thank you for the food **you** made."

Turn the word "thank you" inward and see what happens. "Thank you for **your** prayer, it was so beautiful". "Thank you for **your** food, it was very tasty". "Please, help me, you do it so well.

Words Matter

Expand on what you're saying "thank you" for, and the word "thank you" starts to carry more power. If you make it more personal, then that person will do it with more passion next time and enjoy doing it more, and maybe just develop a love for it!

We should not be afraid to use more words when complimenting others. It makes a substantial difference in the lives of the people around us.

Say "Thank you, that cup of coffee was extremely nice" and next time you might get an extra spoonful of love with your cup of coffee or even get it faster than normal.

No, I'm not saying you should lie, and yes, if need be, we must address people when something is wrong, or out of place. But when it is deserved, give that compliment, and go the extra mile to do so. Complimenting someone and making them feel better, is never a waste of time. It is a seed that can grow and help someone stand taller, in time of need or when compliments are in short supply.

The seeds you have planted can help in times when someone's self-esteem has taken a knock and wants to crack. Think of the glass full of good and bad. The more good compliments there are in the glass. The less space there is for bad words. The good will keep the bad out. Wouldn't you rather help keep someone's glass full of the good stuff?

Words Matter

Compliments can cancel insults that were used against us over the years, or the compliment can even prevent that the insult do harm at all. Restoring balance to us and renewing confidence so that we can learn to love ourselves again.

So, it is not only important to give a compliment, but also to accept one, when it is given to you and enjoy it. It will bring love back to us, not only for yourself but for others. If you can love yourself better, you can love God and others better too. Let your words complement and encourage others and accept when others compliment and encourage you!

Matthew 22:37-39

And he said to him, "You shall love the Lord your God. with all your heart and with all your soul and with all your mind. 38 This is the great and first commandment.39And a second is like it: You shall love your neighbour as yourself.

What are the key takeaways from this chapter?

1. Compliment
2. Give a compliment it can enrich a life.
3. Please and thank you matters.
4. Make it personal.
5. Compliments is never a waste of time.
6. Compliments are seeds we plant that can help when self-esteem is down.
7. Accept a compliment.
8. Pro 3:27 Do not withhold good from those to whom it is due, when it is in your power to do it.

Notes

DEUTERONOMY 31:6

Be strong and courageous. **Do not fear** or be in dread of them, **For it is the LORD your** GOD who goes with you. **He will not leave you** or forsake you."

Chapter 10
The Helper

Genesis 2:18
Then the LORD God said, "It is not good that the man should be alone; I will make him a helper fit for him."

THE HELPER. When God created the helper, **He had something special in mind.** An Assistant, Associate, Supporter, Partner, Collaborator. Two are better than one. Like it or not, women were created as helpers. A fact you cannot change even if you want to. The only thing you are doing is making yourself unhappy, going against God's will. Going against God's word is always a bad idea. Women were made as helpers for men!

In God's Word, women are reminded that we were made as a helper. But women forget that so easily

Words Matter

and like to use their words to get their way instead of helping. Women are good at intimidating and manipulating with words to get their way.

Women, wives, mother, no matter what word is used to describe the helper, it is a big part of the female identity to help. Women were made strong and courageous in His image, more powerful than we know.

Proverbs 31:26

She opens her mouth with wisdom, and the teaching of kindness is on her tongue.

God said. "I have called you by name, you are mine." Yes, we were made as a helper for the man, and that is why we are so exceptional. Men's punishment in the Garden of Eden was heavy, and for that, they needed a helper. From the beginning, God knew men would need help to carry the load, and so also linked our punishment to them.

Genesis 3:16 KJV

Unto the woman he said, I will greatly multiply thy sorrow and thy conception; in sorrow, thou shalt bring forth children; and thy desire shall be to thy husband, and he shall rule over thee.

Proverbs 31 describes women so beautifully, and that is what we should aspire to be but, we tend to forget the strength we have. We must use our words to inspire and build up, not tear down. The words of a woman to her husband, carry more power than she will ever realise.

Words Matter

Proverbs 31:10-12

An excellent wife who can find? She is far more precious than jewels. 11 The heart of her husband trusts in her, and he will have no lack of gain. 12 She does him good, and not harm, all the days of her life.

As helpers, women must also build up, strengthen, and support with their words. Women have a special talent for words and must use them correctly. God has made us strong, bold and inspiring. A partner to assist when needed. Help him stand strong, be there for him when he needs you, supporting him.

Unfortunately, this is not what a lot of women use their words for. Women do not realise the power that lies in their words.

What must be realised here, is not to get stuck on the fact that women were made as helpers, but that help is needed. Why do we need to help? Because from the beginning God knew they would need us. God created women with that in His heart and so gave women a sense of purpose.

God made women to help to support. That's why it is so hurtful when the one that is supposed to help, do the opposite. Instead of using words to strengthen and build up, the helpers use the words that God has blessed her with to tear down.

If the one who should help you stand strong, pushes you down, it is the most overwhelming

Words Matter

pain you can get. Why do you think it is called heartbreak when you lose love or get hurt by a loved one? Those who use the power of the tongue so frivolously will be held responsible, for their every word.

So, let's talk about our words towards our husbands, the man in your life. Look, I'm all for a woman who stands strong and tall but, doing a man's work for him is not the way. Taking control away from him is a bad idea.

You're his supporter, his support system. Stop using your words to take the control out of his hands and let him lead you! Your words should support him not undermine him.

Stand strong, use your words, speak up, and make clear what is on your mind, talk to him but do not manipulate him. Use clear and honest words. Speak from your heart. You can open your heart, it's good for you! Just always remember how you say it matters.

Use words of love and support and no, just saying what is on your mind "I say what I think" doesn't mean that you're just a straightforward person. It means you're rude and only care about yourself not about what your words can do to others. You can still be honest without being rude or insensitive.

"But I can be honest with my husband" Of course, you must be honest but, just because it is your opinion, doesn't make it right. It just makes it your

Words Matter

honest conclusion. Be considerate with your words and how you deliver them, matters.

Our words and actions on those words, carry power. You can't say, years later that your husband doesn't have control over his own house, if you stole his power from the start with your words. Use your words to be supporting and encouraging. Be his helper, not someone who will take his power from him!

You will be amazed at how strong he is if you start listening to his words and opinions, and not drain them out with your, words and criticism.

Instead of accusing him of never being there for you, calm down. Think before you speak, and instead of accusing him tell him you need him, you need and want his help. Share your heart.

If he hears the words that he is never there for you enough, he may just disappear before your eyes one day. Words carry power especially when it comes from a loved one, because there is more trust involved.

Think before you speak. Stop hurting the people you love with your words, stop hurting anyone with your words. Submit to your husband.

Submitting to God brings us to our knees before God, which is an important part of our spiritual life. If we cannot even be merciful and submit to our earthly other half, how will we be able to submit fully to God?

Words Matter

Be on your knees, humble before God, and you will be able to submit, as a helper, the way God intended it to be.

1Thessaionians 5:11
Therefore encourage one another and build one another up, just as you are doing.

What are the key takeaways from this chapter?
1. The Helper.
2. The Woman was made as a helper.
3. Going against God's plan is a bad idea.
4. Women are good at using their words to get their way.
5. Women were made strong so that they could help.
6. A Wife's words to her husband carry a lot of power.
7. The Helper must build up and support.
8. Being torn down by the one who is supposed to help you, is called heartbreak for a reason.
9. Stop using your words to take control out of his hands.
10. Be considerate in your words.
11. Stop stealing his power with your words.
12. Submit your words to God.
13. Two are better than one.
14. Pro 25:24 It is better to live in a corner of the housetop than in a house shared with a quarrelsome wife.

Notes

Proverbs 12:22

Lying lips are an abomination to

The LORD,

but those who act faithfully

Are His Delight.

Chapter 11
LYING
Luke 16:10
"One who is faithful in a very little is also faithful in much, and one who is dishonest in a very little is also dishonest in much.

Lying is no little thing, but if we can't be trusted to be honest, how can we be trusted with more? Our words are meant to be beautiful and refreshing to hear, not full of deception and lies, our words should carry hope and love, not gloom and pain.

There is no good reason to lie. Lying is bad! There is no such thing as lying, for a good reason. Lying is lying and cannot be used for good. No good can come of it. Don't ever think or say that if you lie

Words Matter

you are doing it for someone's good. No one likes being lied to.

Not only is it against God's law for a good reason, but the truth will always come out. Then the damage is more, and the betrayal then hurts so much more if it is found out in another way than you being honest.

Here is the thing with lying. You are deceitful, the trust and confidence that someone gave you, or that someone wants to give you, is destroyed. And getting trust back is so much more difficult than when you didn't have to earn it. But was given because you started with a clean slate. Lying can cause a lot of harm.

If you think the truth never comes out, you are lying to yourself thinking that no one knows the truth. Or you've gotten so good at lying that it might take people longer to figure it out, which means you're very good at a bad thing. Doing a bad thing good, is very bad. In other words, don't lie.

Ephesians 4:25
Therefore, having put away falsehood, let each one of you speak the truth with his neighbour, for we are members one of another.

Omitting the truth is also lying. "I didn't lie, I just did not tell you". Who has ever heard those words? And did you feel like you weren't lied to? Acting falsely is still lying.

Words Matter

It's the same with twisting words, leaving out words here and there, so that you only have to tell half of the truth, and the person you are talking to only understands a part of it. Telling only part of the story is lying.

Leaving out something, of what you are supposed to say, to benefit you or because you think it is better not to tell the complete story, is not only lying but deceitful. Wanting to save someone's feelings is an honourable thing to do, but lying is not the way. Your words mean something, and what they mean is up to you.

I found this free book-reading app online. Only after downloading the app, I found out that the app is free, and not the books you want to read. They will give you a chapter or two for free, but the rest is not free. The advertisement is for a **free book-reading** app, but they make sure to phrase it correctly so that it has a double meaning.

Phrasing the words just right is an old sales technique, but it is still lying, no matter what the reason is behind the framing of the lie. Even when you say it just right so that it can have more than one meaning, it still makes it a lie because in your heart that is what you intended to do! It is unfortunate to see that people also do this in their personal lives, not only for financial reasons.

A lie is a lie, there is no such thing as half a lie or half the truth. Even if to spare someone's feelings. Just leaving out a word here or there does not

Words Matter

change the fact that you are lying. The same counts for small and big lies, and a white lie. There is no such thing. Lying is lying no matter the reason colour or size.

Luke 12:2-3
Nothing is covered up that will not be revealed, or hidden that will not be known. 3 Therefore whatever you have said in the dark shall be heard in the light, and what you have whispered in private rooms shall be proclaimed on the housetops.

Zechariah 8:16
These are the things that you shall do Speak the truth to one another; render in your gates judgments that are true and make for peace.

What are the key takeaways from this chapter?

1. Lying.
2. If you cannot be trusted in telling the truth, how can God trust you with bigger things?
3. There is no good reason for lying.
4. Doing a bad thing well is bad.
5. Omitting the truth is still lying.
6. Trust lost is not easy to get back.
7. Saying something just right so it has more than one meaning is lying.
8. There is no such thing as half a lie or half of the truth, and no big lie or small lie; lying is lying.
9. That which is covered up will be revealed.
10. Pro 12:22 Lying lips are an abomination to the LORD, but those who act faithfully are his delight.

Notes

--*Mark 10:45*--

For even the Son of Man
CAME NOT TO BE SERVED BUT TO SERVE,
and to give his life
as a ransom for many.

CHAPTER 12
At your Service

Hebrews 13:2
Do not neglect to show hospitality to strangers, for thereby some have entertained angels unawares.

Colossians 4:5-6
Walk in wisdom toward outsiders, making the best use of the time. 6 Let your speech always be gracious, seasoned with salt, so that you may know how you ought to answer each person.

Are you ready to serve all God's children? The customer is always right. A phrase everyone in the service industry knows and dislikes. Even if we never say it out loud and the words are only in our minds, we need to fix how we approach this.

Words Matter

Have you ever considered that it's only a simple fact to phrase the words correctly when speaking to a customer? Making the entire conversation turn out better and fixing the problem.

Working in the service industry it is easy to forget that we do not only work with customers but people. People acting the way they do because they feel cheated, done in, or manipulated.

If you approach your customers with the right attitude, that the customer **is** always right, and realise that they are also a child of God just like you, the right words will come on their own to make them feel at ease with you. But if you are going to come with an attitude of the customer, **must** always be right, because "they pay my salary", then your words are not going to come out right, because your attitude is not right.

You will find it difficult to work with them. Pay close attention to the one word in the sentence that has changed.

The customer **is** always right.

The customer **must** always be right.

One word can make a huge difference to the outcome of a conversation. Even if you only say it in your mind. Whether it is with a customer, a work colleague, a friend, family, or your children. It can change the whole situation from bad to good. When you fix your words.

Now, think about it for a moment are we not all busy with customer service all day? When we

Words Matter

interact with anyone, we are busy representing either good or bad, so who do you represent, God or the devil?

If someone comes to you with a bad attitude because they are hurting and feel they have been done in, taken advantage of, or harmed by someone else, and now take it out on you. Are you going to help and serve them with a good and loving approach or are you going to treat them with the same attitude as they have been giving you? Are you going to make sure your words are just as harmful to them as their words have been to you? Or are you going to treat them the way a child of God should?

Just because you think someone has sin in their lives because of the way they act does not make them less of a child of God, no one is perfect. It doesn't mean you can treat them with less love, in fact, they need more.

Proverbs 15:4

A gentle tongue is a tree of life, but perverseness in it breaks the spirit.

Are you going to have a customer **is** always right attitude, or a customer **must** always be right attitude? Will you change one word in your attitude to be of better service to God?

Remember most people with a bad attitude are that way because something happened that made them that way. If we serve God well, we will be able to help with the healing of the hearts of God's children by always treating them with loving words.

This does not mean that we should allow people to walk over us, mistreat us, and talk to us as they want to because we are children of God. You can put a stop to that without having the same bad attitude as them. More bad attitude won't fix anything.

So, who are you at service to? Are you ready to be of service to God or only when the person God sends along your path is nice to you?

Are you at service to all or only to those who are not acting out because they have been mistreated, misused, and misunderstood?

Jesus came to be of service to us. Are you still willing to be of service to Him or only when it is nice and friendly people, He sends your way to be helped?

When you change your attitude from "**He** is being rude to me." To "**Why** is he being rude" the outcome will also change. Changing one word in your attitude will make all the difference so are you ready to be at service to God?

Matthew 25:35–40

For I was hungry, and you gave me food, I was thirsty, and you gave me drink, I was a stranger and you welcomed me, 36 I was naked and you clothed me, I was sick, and you visited me, I was in prison, and you came to me.' 37 Then the righteous will answer Him, saying, 'Lord, when

Words Matter

did we see you hungry and feed you, or thirsty and give you drink? 38 And when did we see you a stranger and welcome you, or naked and clothe you? 39 And when did we see you sick or in prison and visit you?' 40 And the King will answer them, 'Truly, I say to you, as you did it to one of the least of these my brothers, you did it to me.'

What are the key takeaways from this chapter?

1. At your service.
2. Serving God's children.
3. Fix your attitude.
4. One word makes a difference.
5. Do you represent good or bad?
6. A Bad attitude doesn't fix a bad attitude.
7. People with bad attitudes are that way for a reason
8. Are you ready to serve God's children or only the nice ones
9. Psa 39:1 I said, "I will guard my ways, that I may not sin with my tongue; I will guard my mouth with a muzzle, so long as the wicked are in my presence."
10. Pro 12:18 There is one whose rash words are like sword thrusts, but the tongue of the wise brings healing.

Notes

Ephesians 6:4

~~Fathers do not provoke your~~

Children

to anger but bring them up

in the discipline and

Instruction of the

Lord

Chapter 13
Children

Proverbs 22:6

Train up a child in the way he should go.
even when he is old, he will not depart from it.

Teach your children to speak correctly and properly. Being young is no excuse for being ill-mannered. Out of the mouth of an infant comes ignorance, not truth. A child is still learning right from wrong, so how can there be truth in their words? They may tell it as they see it, but that does not make it true or acceptable. If they have the ability to say something out of place, they can be taught that it is out of place and why.

Words Matter

As parents, it is our responsibility to teach our children to speak correctly and also why.

The truth will come from the infant's mouth, is perhaps an old familiar saying. But just because it seems true to the child does not make it so and does not make negative words hurt less.

There is a time and place for everything in life and the right way and time to say it counts a lot and we need to teach this to our children.

Being able to use your words correctly is very important to learn. If we can teach our children to use it correctly from an early age, just think what an advantage we give them. Then they don't have to learn it later in life when it is already a part of their everyday expressions.

Our children's words are our responsibility. Will you think it's funny if your child says a swear word? The same thing counts for saying something out of place. It is our job as parents to find out where and why they learned it and put a stop to it. Then teach them right from wrong, do not just let it be. There is a time and place for children to talk, and it is your job as parents to teach them this. Some words and conversations are not made for our children's ears.

We as parents have the responsibility to protect them from that. But when they do hear it and use it, we have to help them and teach them, why it is bad, and what harm it can do if used incorrectly.

Words Matter

Words are a much bigger part of our lives than we realise. If you are not going to take the time to talk to your child, how will they ever learn what the right and wrong words are and how to use them?

That means you're also going to have to talk to them properly. Make time to really talk to your children. Let them learn the right way from you, and don't always be abrupt and rushed when you talk to them.

If you don't talk to them correctly, how can you expect them to talk correctly to other people, now and in the future? They should learn from you which words carry value and how they should be used.

Unfortunately, nowadays, we as parents are not the only people who play a role in our children's lives. But it remains our job to teach them to speak correctly and stop the poor phrasing when they pick it up from outside their homes.

Bend the tree while it's still young. If we don't teach our children the right words to use now, just think what damage their words will do when they are adults, because of their ignorance.

Just think about the damage your words have already done to others as a result of your ignorance about words as an adult, because you did not know how wrong it was. Do you want your children to do that type of damage if you can teach them the right way now? Our children are the future learn them the correct words now.

Words Matter
Deuteronomy 4:9
Only be on your guard and diligently watch yourselves, so that you do not forget the things your eyes have seen, and so that they do not slip from your heart as long as you live. Teach them to your children and grandchildren.

What are the key takeaways from this chapter?

1. Children.
2. Out of the mouth of an infant comes ignorance, not truth.
3. Teach your child to speak correctly.
4. Teach them right from wrong.
5. Negative words are still painful, even from a child.
6. Learning the right words as a child is better. Ignorance does damage
7. Our children's words are our responsibility.
8. There is a time and place for children to talk.
9. Make time to really talk to your children.
10. Pro 20:11 Even a child makes himself known by his acts, by whether his conduct is pure and upright.

Notes

(Psalms 23:4-5)

Even though I walk through the valley **of the shadow of death,** I will fear no evil, for you are with me, **your rod and your staff,** they comfort me. ₅**You prepare a table before me** in the presence. of my enemies, **you anoint my head with oil**. my cup overflows.

Chapter 14
"Shout to the lord"
Joshua 6:16
And at the seventh time, when the priests had blown the trumpets, Joshua said to the people, "Shout, for the LORD has given you the city.

With a shout, GOD gave the city of Jericho into the hands of His people. How many shouts do you have for the Lord? We shout a lot inside about all the concerns in our lives and the world around us. Our internal struggles sometimes get too much and then come out. We use our words in so many ways to get rid of our frustrations or struggles with the world and its people, and all that we must experience and are exposed to. However, we must remember that words hurt whether they are thrown inward or outwardly, within ourselves or to someone else.

Words Matter

If we can learn to turn our shouts to God, not at Him but to Him then He will give us the victory also! Before our war of words makes a shout into the world, we must share it with God first.

Talk to Him, shout, if you must, and in Him, we will get the victory. The words that we shout carry power, and when it is thrown out there into the world, they do more harm than we ever know or realise, which was never the intention. In the end, we just finally needed to let it go to get rid of the frustration.

But once it's out, it can't be taken back. Once the words are out, the damage is done. Simply saying sorry, "I didn't mean it; I was tired or frustrated" will not undo the damage your words just did. Give your tired to the Lord give your frustration to the Lord and your shout will not escape to the wrong person. God will give you the victory!

Matthew 11:28-30

Come to me, all who labour and are heavy. laden, and I will give you rest. 29 Take my yoke upon you, and learn from me, for I am gentle and lowly in heart, and you will find rest for your souls. 30 For my yoke is easy, and my burden is light."

Give it to God. Let Him sort it out. Shout it out to the Lord! God is our healer and saviour. He can carry it, we just have to give it to Him that's why He died on the cross. Talk to Him and ask Him to help! **Just let go and let God**!

Words Matter

God's timing on when things happen is just so much better than our timing, God will give you the victory and then you will shout for joy. We don't even have to walk around a city 7 times to get our victory! All we need to do is turn to Him. All we need to do is *let go and let God have control.*

Shout to the Lord.

If we can learn to give our shouts of sorrow to God. We must also remember to give our shout of triumph to God after He has given the victory in our hands and shout out the victory to the world.

Use your words and testify of the victory. Tell the world what God has done for you and shout the joy out into the world. We need to use our words of praise and worship to thank God for the victory. For the victory belongs to the Lord.

Philippians 4:6-7

Do not be anxious about anything but in everything by prayer and supplication With Thanksgiving let your requests be made known to God. 7 And the peace of God, which surpasses all understanding, will guard your hearts and your minds in Christ Jesus.

When the peace that surpasses all understanding rests upon you. You will have peace even in times of trouble, then you will know God has given you eternal victory. Then your shouts will always be victorious, and no evil forces or things of the world will be able to separate you from the victory in God's love.

No matter how many types of shouts there are, and who sees a shout as what, or what the world thinks a shout means, anger, happiness, frustration or victory. It's about the reaction that lives in our hearts, and to let it go fully and utterly, and when we can give all our shouts to God, only the victory shouts will remain.

James 1:2-4

Count it all joy, my brothers, when you meet trials of various kinds, 3 for you know that the testing of your faith produces steadfastness. 4 And let steadfastness have its full effect, that you may be perfect and complete, lacking in nothing.

What are the key takeaways from this chapter?

1. Shout to the Lord.
2. Our struggles turn into shouts.
3. Give your shout to the Lord.
4. The Lord gives the victory.
5. Let go and let God.
6. God's timing for victory is perfect.
7. Shout out the victory, shout for joy.
8. The peace that surpasses all understanding comes with the eternal shout of victory.
9. Psa 33:3 Sing to him a new song; play skillfully on the strings, with loud shouts.

Notes

Psalms 62:2

HE ALONE IS MY ROCK

And my salvation,

MY FORTRESS.

I shall not be greatly shaken.

Chapter 15
Build on the rock
Luke 6:47-48
Everyone who comes to me and hears my words and does them, I will show you what he is like 48 he is like a man building a house, who dug deep and laid the foundation on the rock. And when a flood arose, the stream broke against that house and could not shake it, because it had been well-built.

The true Cornerstone. If we build our life on the Word of God, we will be building on solid rock, and so it will be if we build our words on the principles of God's Word. He has given us many examples in His Word to follow. Words full

Words Matter

of love, joy, peace, patience, kindness, goodness, faithfulness, humility, and self-control.

Our lives are nothing else than this. A house built by our daily words. Every stone we pack and every word we use, brings us to our end product. The question is who is your cornerstone and are you building on the rock, or are you building on the sand? Is your foundation strong enough to keep your house standing, or will your selfish words to others be your downfall, and sink your house one day? Will all your impure words let your house fall?

1Peter 2:6-8

For it stands in scripture: "Behold, I am laying in Zion. a stone, a cornerstone chosen and precious, and whoever believes in him will not be put to shame"7 So the honour is for you who believe, but for those who do not believe, "the stone that the builders rejected has become the cornerstone,"8 and "a stone of stumbling, and a rock of offense. "They stumble. Because they disobey the word, as they were destined to do.

Everything we do in our lifetime is building towards our destination. Whether it is learning from our mistakes or taking the road less travelled. We do it to build towards our destination. It is the same for the words we use to construct the buildings in our lives. The more time we spend in the Word of God, the more we will start to speak like the Word

Words Matter

of God, and that's a couple of good building blocks to have.

Have you ever noticed that a loving couple who have been together for a long time start to speak and think the same? Why do you think that is? Because of all the time they spend together.

When you spend more time in the Word of God and more time speaking to Him, you will start thinking and speaking in His ways. Is it not better that we use our words the way God intended for us to use them and learn how to use them from God's Word?

The correct words and ways we need to build our destination are in the Word of God. Every word we use leads to how people see us and what they think of us. Even if it doesn't matter what the world thinks, for only God's opinion matters, and He sees the true us. What does matter is how people see the children of God, and what we say and do reflects in our lives.

But if we are building with the true cornerstone, it will enable us to show the world that building on the rock is the only way to get to the wonderful destination God has planned for us. Showing the world there is only one true cornerstone. When our building blocks are all good, pure, and uplifting, we will have a strong and more stable building at the end of our destination, that stands on the only true rock. So, make sure your words will serve as good building blocks.

Words Matter

Proverbs 11:9

With his mouth, the godless man would destroy his neighbour, but by knowledge, the righteous are delivered.

Proverbs 15:4

A gentle tongue is a tree of life, but perverseness in it breaks the spirit.

What are the key takeaways from this chapter?

1. Build on the rock!
2. The true Cornerstone.
3. A house built out of your words.
4. Everything we do and say in our lives is building towards our Destination.
5. The more time we spend in the Word of God, the more we will speak like the Word of God.
6. Learn from God's word.
7. Pro 11:11 By the blessing of the upright a city is exalted, but by the mouth of the wicked it is overthrown.

Notes

Notes

Matthew 21:21

And **Jesus** answered **them,** "**Truly**, I say to you if you have **faith** and do not **doubt,** you **will** not only **do** what has **been** done **to** the **fig** tree, **but** even **if** you say to **this mountain**, 'Be **taken** up and **thrown** into **the sea**,' it **will Happen**.

Chapter 16
Faith in words
Hebrews 11:1-3

Now faith is the assurance of things Hoped for, the conviction of things not seen. 2 For by it the people of old received their commendation 3 By faith, we understand that the universe. Was created by the word of God, so that what is seen was not made out of things that are visible.

Words are hollow without faith. Your faith in words carries the power in your life. At the end of the day, you have to realise that you have the power to accept and reject words. It doesn't matter what gracious or arrogant words are spoken about you or to you; if you do not believe it, it cannot carry power in your lives.

Words Matter

Words spoken into our lives can be blessings or afflictions. But it only has power if we believe it. With words, it happens more unconsciously than we realise.

If someone tells you that what you have done or made is extraordinary, and that you are going to make and do more wonderful things in your life.

It is very easy to believe before you think about what has been said, because it comes from someone else's point of view.

Then your faith in it will be stronger if it is confirmed by someone else. But unfortunately, our faith in it can also suffer. If only one person, from the majority, says something bad, like I don't think it's that good or I've seen better. We would rather believe the negative one.

Unfortunately, we have a way of believing the negative words rather than the good ones. Bad words that people speak in our lives can become an affliction to us.

We need to send those bad words out of our lives immediately. Ask God to deafen your ears and hearts to it. We need to deal with it and, in the name of Jesus, send those words from our lives.

Every time someone tells you something that makes you feel you're not good enough or makes you feel unworthy, you need to sort it out.

All those little rejections will build up, then it only takes one or two bad little words to send you over

Words Matter

the top and it becomes an ailment that makes you feel unworthy and inferior, or even worse.

If you believe it, it will inflame and damage everything in your life. Especially if you start to feel overwhelmed and try to shift that burden or responsibility onto others. When the weight of it becomes too much for you to handle alone, you may be tempted to offload it onto someone else, rather than facing it head-on.

It will end up on people around you and close to you. It's a vicious circle of bad words all around you that will start affecting the people you love. Your faith in those bad words can make or break you.

Think of it like this: you are an empty glass. If you hear all day and every day that you are not good enough and you cannot do anything right, your glass will start to overflow with all those bad words, and those words will overflow onto the people around you and start to affect them too.

So, it will go on from person to person until everyone in and around your life is affected. But if you can throw those words out of your life and not allow them to fill your glass and leave only the good words in your glass. Only the good ones will then come out and spill over onto others.

If you believe in the good words that people have said in your life, your glass will overflow with all the good. That's something you want to let spill over. You must let your faith stand strong in what

Words Matter

you know to be the truth of yourself. You know who you are and what your truth is.

Put your faith in God. Let Him show you the words you should take in. So, when the bad words are thrown in your direction, you throw them away and ask God to take them out of your heart and mind and accept the healing in the name of Jesus. There is no stronger word than the name of Jesus. The true Word which came to us to die for us.

Put your faith in the good words that God has sent into your life and accept them over your life. Do not believe the bad words because bad things do not come from God.

John 14:13-16

Whatever you ask in my name, this I will do that the Father may be glorified in the Son 14 If you ask me anything. in my name, I will do it. 15 "If you love me, you will keep my commandments. 16 And I will ask the Father, and he will give you another Helper, to be with you forever,

John 15:7

If you abide in me, and my words abide in you, ask whatever you wish, and it will be done for you.

Colossians 3:17

And whatever you do, in word or deed, do everything in the name of the Lord Jesus, giving thanks to God the Father through Him.

Words Matter

What are the key takeaways from this chapter?

1. Faith in words.
2. Words are hollow without faith.
3. If you do not believe the words, they cannot affect you.
4. We believe bad words more than good words.
5. The bad words people leave in our lives will spill over onto others.
6. Know what your truth is.

Notes

Psalms 119:145-147

With my whole Heart

I cry; answer me, o Lord! I will keep

your statutes.

146 I call to you; save me, that I may

observe your testimonies. 147 I rise before

dawn and cry for help.

I hope in your words. Are we still able to

Serve God?

Chapter 17
Answer the call
Isaiah 6:9-10

9 And he said, "Go, and say to this people: "'Keep on hearing, but do not understand. keep on seeing, but do not perceive.' 10 Make the heart of this people dull, and their ears heavy, and blind their eyes: lest they see with their eyes and hear with their ears and understand. with their hearts and turn and be healed."

Call= cry from the heart
Hear= be made aware
Listen= give one's attention

Do we still hear when God's children call for help? Do we still listen to the call of the heart? We still ask God to make us serviceable for Him to employ us for His work that still needs to be done here on earth!

Words Matter

"Lord here I am, use me for your purpose."
But when was the last time you thought about the fact that when you call out to God in prayer for help, He sends someone your way to help you? When someone else calls out to God in prayer, He may send you on their way to help them. So, do you still hear the call? Do you still answer if He sends someone to you with a call for help?

Isaiah 6:8
And I heard the voice of the Lord saying, "Whom shall I send, and who will go for us?" Then I said, "Here I am! Send me."

Every day, all around us, God's beloved children are crying out for help with their words, but we listen and hear nothing. Their words betray what is going on in their hearts, but our ears have gone deaf.
"How are you?"
"I had a rough week!"
But do we still ask why, or do we just say, Oh, it's not nice? Sometimes, someone just needs to talk to get it out of their hearts, they just need someone to hear them, someone to understand, not act, just understand. Someone who just knows what is in their hearts and how they feel.
"How are you? "
"Oh, ok, just didn't sleep very well!"
Maybe God will send that person your way because of his prayer this morning, which was: "Help me

Words Matter

sleep better Lord." You may have also had trouble sleeping recently but have already figured out how to fix it, you already have the answer they need, or He wants the two of you to sit down together and work on the solution. Because your prayer this morning was the same, and you can't sleep either, but together you can find a solution.

Isaiah 55:8-9

For my thoughts are not your thoughts, neither are your ways my ways, declares the LORD. 9 For as the heavens are higher than the earth, so are my ways higher than your ways and my thoughts than your thoughts.

There are giveaways in people's words everywhere that we miss because we no longer hear the call of the heart. How many times have you listened to what someone has to say but preferred not to hear? Because you didn't feel like getting involved with it, or thought he was just whining again or just talking to have something to say?

How many times do you choose not to respond to someone's words because now is not convenient for you to pay attention to them? Or you think that person always has the same story?

What if that was the person God wanted you to help today? Have you ever thought that if they can finally talk to someone about it maybe it won't be the same story over and over again because they can finally share it with someone?

Words Matter

Everyone around us has small calls in their words all day. But do we still hear it, or do we prefer not to hear it?

If only we could learn to hear and not just listen but to really hear. Will we then even be able to hear the **call** in their words? We still listen to what people say, but we don't hear the words.

The call for deliverance.

The call of solitude.

The call for the father's heart.

The call for more love, care, and peace.

The call for help!

The needs and desires of the world and our loved ones lie so openly in their words, but we no longer hear them. We have forgotten how to hear the call because for so long we chose not to hear all those who cry out in their soul.

Have you ever thought God put us in a certain place at a certain time so that we could answer a call? But then we still miss it. We are so eager to help promote God's kingdom and to do great things for Him, but we miss hearing what is right under our noses.

How many times have we prayed "God use me where you need me" but then missed a call to help from God's children? Because we want to make a big difference, we miss the things around us where we can make a difference right now. Start listening to the words of the people around you.

"How are you doing today?"

Words Matter

"Okay, thanks, and you?"

"I am glad to hear that!"

But you didn't hear. You didn't even listen. It's just okay, not good. Why just okay? Ask why, listen, and act if you can. Let them know you are there for them.

If everyone just starts hearing one person's words today, and every day, really listen and hear the call in their words and their hearts and do something about it. Even if it's not to act but just to be there for them. How much extra love is going out there every day? Even if it's just talking to them about it and showing them love and support.

What a big difference it will make in and to the kingdom of God with all that extra love out there. Is the greatest commandment not love? How much extra love can we show to people not only with our words but also by listening to their words, really listening?

What a difference we will make if we don't just listen to people's words but start to hear them? Listen to the call in their words. Listen to the call in their hearts.

We are here but away. Our eyes mist up and become blind to the things around us, our ears hear but understand nothing. So, how will we still hear the voice of the children of God, if we have gone deaf and blind to the things of the world?

How will you hear the call of their hearts? Where will your helping hand go? If you just stare in

astonishment at the call of their hearts. *Are you still willing to be of service?*
For the call that God wants you to answer?
For what God calls you for?
Are you still willing to do what still needs to be done all around you? Or do you only want to do the big things? Are a lot of little things not better than a big thing?

Matthew 9:37-38
Then he said to His disciples, "The harvest is plentiful, but the labourers are few,[38] *therefore, pray earnestly to the Lord of the harvest to send out labourers into His harvest."*

What are the key takeaways from this chapter?
1. Answer the call.
2. Do you still hear the call?
3. Lord how can I help today?
4. God sends people for us to help.
5. We only hear what we want to hear.
6. Listen with your heart.
7. Sometimes someone just needs to talk.
8. We are eager to help God's kingdom, but we miss what is right under our noses.
9. Show them love.
10. Show them understanding.
11. Who did God send to you today?
12. Did you hear the call?
13. Did you answer?

Notes

Ephesians 5:4
Let there be No
filthiness
nor foolish talk
nor crude joking,
which are out of place,
But instead, let there
Be thanksgiving.

Words Matter

Chapter 18
Just a Joke

Proverbs 26:18-19
Like a madman who throws firebrands, arrows, and death. 19 Is the man who deceives his neighbour and says, "I am only joking!"

Jokes can be good, they can lighten up a room, change the atmosphere, even make a weird and awkward moment relaxed or pleasant humour can disarm people, but joking, like everything else in life, has a time and place. When it comes to joking, there are a few do's and don'ts.

Never say it's just a joke, never get personal, never badmouth people, or insult them and choose your audience carefully. To name just a few.

If you see a reason to declare that it's just a joke, you already realise that what you said might not

Words Matter

be that funny. That someone may feel offended by it. So, why do it then? Is it that you are maybe trying to avoid an uncomfortable silence? Do you want to lighten the mood, or do you want to hurt and put someone down? What are your motives?

Maybe you feel uncertain about what you just said. I've heard people say "It's just a joke" before the offended person even reacts. Meaning they know exactly what they just said and did!

No matter the reason for the joke. The problem with it is that. The words have already been said. You can't take them back. You can't make the words disappear.

Stop saying "It's just a joke" to try and make it better, on the contrary, you make it worse.

Now you are just drawing more attention to what you said, because you did not just say it, you emphasize it by adding "just a joke". You just added that you know your words were nasty and wrong, but you still preferred to say it.

Why bring it up in the first place if you do not want to stand behind your words? Clearly, it's not a joke because there's nothing funny about it. If someone thought it was funny you wouldn't need to say it. Because their laughing will make it clear! The fact that you cannot put a guard in front of your mouth to stop you from saying the wrong thing does not mean you can now suddenly pretend it is funny. **No one believes it**. Thinking

Words Matter

before you speak is not just a thought; it should be second nature! A way of life!

Psalms 141:3

Set a guard, O LORD, over my mouth; keep watch over the door of my lips!

Just because someone laughs at your joke, doesn't mean your words do not hurt them. It simply means they are mature enough and do not need to show you that your words offended them, and sometimes it is not worth bringing it up. Hurting someone is never funny.

You and that person may have a good sense of humour with each other, and that person may not even realise that it is happening, but you are planting seeds! Your bad joke is a seed you are planting. Even if it was truly just a joke.

Galatians 6:7-8

Do not be deceived: God is not mocked, for whatever one sows, that will he also reap. 8 For the one who sows to his own, flesh will from the flesh reap corruption, but the one who sows to the Spirit will from the Spirit reap eternal life.

If the person is spiritually strong enough, they will not be affected, but even the spiritually strong people also have their off and weak days. Are you willing to take the risk of not knowing if it will affect them today? Even if they think it doesn't bother them, that seed is planted. Seeds that will be watered by someone with bad intentions, who

Words Matter

will use the same words to add doubt. That way your seeds will be watered, again and again by others. Even by you when you joke again over the same thing. The seeds you planted will grow until the joke is not funny anymore, but painful.

Have you ever heard how two different people tell the same joke? With one it seems funny and with the other, it sounds rude. Make sure you are not one of those people who sounds offensive when he tells a joke. Some people should rather stay away from jokes in order not to hurt others' feelings with the wording of a joke. Remember just because you say it is a joke does not mean someone will believe you.

Let's put the joking aside for a moment and talk about laughing. Be careful who and what you laugh at. People may share their deep hearts, and words they have hidden for a long time with you. Make sure they are not talking seriously from the heart before you start to laugh. Remember, just because you think it's funny doesn't mean you can laugh about it. You might not have heard the whole story. You might laugh at something that wasn't meant as a joke at all but is ultimately a very serious problem. Make sure it's a joke; wait, listen.

You will miss the final point they wanted to make because you didn't finish listening to their words. You found the beginning so funny that you made your deduction and then laughed about something

Words Matter

that's not funny at all. People will sometimes start a story one way, so that they can systematically get to the point, that you can see the big picture. But you will never see the big picture if you laugh it off when the conversation has only started.

Listen before you just laugh. Think before you do. Just because it sounds ridiculous to you, does not mean it is. That's simply because you didn't finish listening! And remember, everyone's point of view is different.

We must think before we act, especially when it comes to words. Whether they are the words in our hearts we share with others, or our reactions to the words of others, whether they are words we receive or words we give out. Your words and actions on words can hurt someone.

Psalms 15:1-5

A Psalm of David. O LORD, who shall sojourn in your tent? Who shall dwell on your holy hill? 2 He who walks blamelessly and does what is right and speaks truth in his heart; 3 who does not slander with his tongue and does no evil to his neighbour, nor takes up a reproach against his friend; 4 In whose eyes a vile person is despised, but who honours those who fear the LORD; who swears to his own hurt and does not change

What are the key takeaways from this chapter?

1. Just a joke.
2. Jokes have a time and place.

Words Matter

3. If you have to say it's just a joke, you know it was not funny.
4. Calling words that offended someone a joke does not erase the words you said.
5. Insulting someone is not funny
6. If you cannot stand behind the words you just said, do not say them.
7. Thinking before you speak should be second nature, a way of life.
8. Your joke is a seed you plant.
9. Your seeds will get watered by others.
10. Not everyone is good at telling jokes.
11. Not everything you think is funny should be laughed at.
12. Your words and actions on words can hurt someone.

Notes

Notes

2 Corinthians 1:20-22

For all the promises of God find their,

Yes, in Him.

That is why it is through Him
That we utter our Amen
to God for His glory.

21 And it is God who establishes us with

you in Christ,

and has anointed us,

22 and who has also put His seal on us

and given us His Spirit in our hearts

AS A GUARANTEE.

Words Matter

Chapter 19
Obedient to God's words

Genesis 12:1-4

Now the LORD said to Abram, "Go from your country and your kindred and your father's house to the land that I will show you. 2And I will make of you a great nation, and I will bless you and make your name great so that you will be a blessing. 3I will bless those who bless you, and him who dishonours you I will curse, and in you all the families of the earth shall be blessed." 4 So Abram went, as the Lord had told him, and Lot went with him. Abram was seventy-five years old when he departed from Haran.

Do we still listen to God's words? When God gave Abraham a command, he did it. He valued God's words. He didn't say but let Sharhi have children first then I will move, or Let's wait

Words Matter

until this or that falls into place then I will move. No, he listened to God's words and did it! Abram was obedient to God's words, and God blessed him for his obedience. Words carry a lot of power, and the words of God carries all the power. The faster we learn to listen to God's words the better our lives will be.

Just look at the promise God gave to Abraham. He believed in the words of God and acted on them. He did not wonder, maybe I heard wrong, or maybe this way would be better. He just did it. Abraham also learned from his mistakes on the way and was afraid when he came to a foreign country, but still, he listened when God told him and did it.

He knew and accepted the power of God's words and obeyed. Not forcing his way, and all of God's promises to him came true. Abraham knew he could trust God and had faith in God's words and plan.

Genesis 22:2-3

He said, "Take your son, your only son Isaac, whom you love, and go to the land of Moriah and offer him there as a burnt offering on one of the mountains of which I shall tell you. 3 So, Abraham rose early in the morning, saddled his donkey and took two of his young men with him, and his son Isaac. And he cut the wood for the burnt offering and arose and went to the place of which God had told him.

Words Matter

There is a reason why the Bible is referred to as the Word of God. God's words and promises are captured for us in it. We will know His voice if we turn to His Word. The more we read the Bible, the more we will get to know God's voice, get to know Him, and hear His words. It can bring His promise into reality in our lives.

The Bible is not just a historical record of sacred scriptures or a set of virtuous laws. It's alive and active it is God's message for us. It is His words, and still carries power today. He is the same yesterday, today and tomorrow.

Hebrews 13:8

Jesus Christ is the same as yesterday and today and forever.

That is why it is still the most read book today. It's God's words. The more we read God's Word the better we will recognize His voice in our day-to-day life and see Him all around us. We will also see and hear His promises to us and if we obey His words, we can make them ours.

There are so many promises for us in His Word, we simply need to start accepting them and start living his words!

Deuteronomy 28:1-2

"And if you faithfully obey the voice of the LORD your God, being careful to do all his commandments that I command you today, the LORD your God will set you high above all the

Words Matter

nations of the earth. 2 And all these blessings shall come upon you and overtake you, if you obey the voice of the LORD your God.

<u>What are the key takeaways from this chapter?</u>
1. Obedient to the Word of God.
2. Value God's words.
3. No questions asked just do it.
4. Trust God's words.
5. God's words and promises are captured for us in His Word, the Bible.
6. He is the same today as yesterday.
7. Accept God's words and start living it.
8. Jas 1:22-23 But be doers of the word, and not hearers only, deceiving yourselves. 23 For if anyone is a hearer of the word and not a doer, he is like a man who looks intently at his natural face in a mirror.

Notes

Notes

Acts 1:5

For John baptized with water, but you will be baptized with the

Holy Spirit

not many days from now.

Chapter 20
Holy Spirit
John 14:26
But the Helper, the Holy Spirit, whom the Father will send in my name, he will teach you all things and bring to your remembrance all that I have said to you.

The Holy Spirit our guide in this temporary dwelling of ours, which we call Home. We must trust Him and allow Him to guide us. For God did not give us a spirit of fear and trouble but He gave us His spirit. We must do everything with the guidance of the Holy Spirit.

The spirit of love, peace, wisdom, encouragement, and consolation. Our words must therefore also be the sign of the spirit of God that lives inside us. Pray every day that God will guide our words and keep us through the day.

Words Matter
Psalms 141:3-4

Set a guard, O LORD, over my mouth. keep watch over the door of my lips! 4Do not let my heart incline to any evil, to busy myself with wicked deeds in company with men who work iniquity, and let me not eat, of their delicacies!

We must let the Holy Spirit take the lead in our lives so He can guide and teach us in our words. Words of love, comfort, words of encouragement, and enlightenment.

If we give in and allow the spirit of truth to guide us and keep and carry our words, we will see amazing results and changes not only in our lives, but in the lives of the people around us, who share in our words. We will see more fulfilled personalities and lives. Not only will our words no longer harm anyone, but they will also begin to build up, enrich, and restore our neighbours.

When we let ourselves be led by the spirit of truth and love, we will begin to use our words more wilfully to encourage people, to lift them up with our words and not tear them down, to build up and comfort people with what we say. It will bring healing and become a reflection of the spirit we carry within us, and we will be a light that shines for God's kingdom.

Acts 13:47

For so the Lord has commanded us, saying, 'I have made you a light for the Gentiles, that you may bring salvation to the ends of the earth.'

Words Matter

People will want to be more in our orbit, in the same light as us, to also get what we have, to follow our example, and to follow the God we serve. The God of truth and love, and then we can help to lead them to the one true light. **So let your words shine.**

John 1:4-5

In Him was life, and the life was the light of men. 5 The light shines in the darkness, and the darkness has not overcome it.

If you let your words shine, you can lead God's children back to the true light. Our words need to show the light that lives in us, so that we are an example of the God we serve, and then we can attract people to God. When we let the Holy Spirit lead our words, our words will always be good and let the people around us feel loved and safe. Even when we must counsel them, they will feel the love and light shine through. Words matter and carry so much power, but when we let the Holy Spirit lead us, it turns out for the good.

Proverbs 16:24

Gracious words are like a honeycomb, sweetness to the soul and health to the body.

What are the key takeaways from this chapter?
1. Holy Spirit.
2. The Holy Spirit is our guide.
3. Our words must be a sign of the spirit in us.
4. Words of love, kindness, and Grace.

Words Matter

5. The results will be amazing.
6. Lives will change.
7. Let your words be the light for God's kingdom.
8. Our words need to show the light in our lives.
9. Let the Holy Spirit lead your words.
10. 1Corinthians 12:7-8 TPT Each believer is given continuous revelation by the Holy Spirit to benefit not just himself but all. 8 For example: The Spirit gives to one the gift of the word of wisdom. To another, the same Spirit gives the gift of the word of revelation, knowledge.

Notes

Notes

Ecclesiastes 4:6

Better is a handful of quietness
than two hands full
of toil and a striving
After wind.

CHAPTER 21
A Time for Words

<u>Ecclesiastes 5:2</u>
Be not rash with your mouth, nor let your heart be hasty to utter a word before God, for God is in heaven and you are on earth. Therefore let your words be few.

Choose with whom you share your words. There is a time and place for everything, and also for, when and where you share your precious words. There's a time to speak up and a time to keep Quiet, and who you are speaking to plays a big role in this. When to speak up and when to hold your words back can make a big difference if you consider who you are speaking with. Who you are sharing with? Unfortunately, we live in a world and a time where people can and will use

Words Matter

your words as a weapon against you. So, choose carefully, speak carefully.

Ecclesiastes 3:7
A time to tear, and a time to sew, a time to keep silence, and a time to speak.

As children of God, we have been given an open, clean, and honest heart. Honesty and sincerity are our first reactions. When we are in a conversation with someone, it is that honest, open, and sincere heart that guides us in our conversation. But that's not necessarily the right thing to do. No, I'm not saying you should become dishonest and start lying, what I'm saying is, that silence is an option when it comes to certain situations.

Proverbs 10:19
When words are many, transgression is not lacking, but whoever restrains his lips is prudent.

Learn when to speak and when not to, learn who to trust your words with, and learn to make better decisions in friends and people you spend time with.

Yes, I realise it is not always in your control who you spend time with, but where it is, do so and choose your words wisely. We must work and have conversations with people we can't always choose. There are also the times we talk to people, strangers who need to be led to God.

These are exactly the times you should choose your words very carefully and wisely even more

Words Matter

so. As for friends, choose very carefully, because it is with them that you are going to share the words in your heart with the most.

Proverbs 29 v 20

Do you see a man who is hasty in his words? There is more hope for a fool than for him.

Avoid getting involved in an intimate discussion with someone you know you cannot trust or someone you don't know well enough to know if they are trustworthy. Unfortunately, this counts for friends as well. Because we only know people in part and never fully, not even our friends.

1 Corinthians 13:9-10

For we know in part, and we prophesy in part, 10 but when the perfect comes, the partial will pass away.

Be careful. When it is someone untrustworthy, and you must be in a conversation with them from time to time, when the conversation becomes personal, or you realise that emotions are now involved. Just be honest and say, "I'd rather not say anything" or "I do not like where this is going" and just walk away.

People who are dishonest or backstabbing have a way of drawing people into a conversation. Before you know it, your words have left your mouth, and then regret always comes too late. Be vigilant and watch your words always. Doing it will get better

Words Matter

over time, and the Holy Spirit will help you if you start listening to Him. Make sure your words are always something you can be proud of.

I am **not** saying never to trust anyone with all your heart and words again, and that there are no honest and sincere people left, and that you can't trust anyone.

There are some amazing children of God all around us, but our words can be twisted and turned by the wrong people at the wrong time to benefit them. So, choose wisely what kind of people you're sharing your words with. Where there is a need, talk to God and share your words with Him.

Proverbs 14:3
By the mouth of a fool comes a rod for his back, but the lips of the wise will preserve them.

The timing of what we say makes an impact as long as keeping quiet does not turn into omitting the truth. Good news can have a better effect, bad news can carry less pain, misunderstandings can be avoided, and words spoken in confidence will be kept confidential. When your timing is right

If you speak out of time, the person you are speaking to may not realise your words are not to be passed on, or someone may misunderstand the intentions of your words because they cannot see from your point of view. You may be seen as rude and insensitive. This brings us back to the point that you must choose who you share your words with.

Words Matter
Ecclesiastes 4:6
Better is a handful of quietness than two hands full of toil and a striving after wind.

What are the key takeaways from this chapter?

1. A time for words.
2. When, where, and with whom you share your words with, have a time and place.
3. Silence is an option.
4. Learn when to speak and when not to.
5. Be careful in sharing your heart's words.
6. Choose your close friends carefully.
7. Walk away before you say something you will regret.
8. The wrong people will twist your words.
9. Speak to God and share your words and heart with Him.
10. Pro 5:2 that you may keep discretion, and your lips may guard knowledge.

Notes

Proverbs 4:23-24

Keep your heart with all vigilance, for from it flow the springs of life. ₂₄ **Put away from you** CROOKED SPEECH AND PUT DEVIOUS TALK Far From You.

Chapter 22
Words and Unforgiveness

Matthew 18:21-22 ASV
Then came Peter and said to him, Lord, how often shall my brother sin against me, and I forgive him? Until seven times? 22 Jesus saith unto him, I say not unto thee, Until seven times; but, Until seventy times seven.

With all the information and knowledge of what words can carry and do to us and others, let us not forget that words must also be forgiven. Even if we do not accept what was said we must remember that forgiveness must go along with the words that hurt us so much and broke our hearts and spirit. It's one thing to forgive the person who

Words Matter

spoke the words, but it's something else to forgive the words that were spoken.

Think for a moment, have you ever heard someone say "I hate those words!" and even you may feel that way when something is being said, a certain word or phrase? If you should ask that person why he doesn't like it, most people won't be able to answer except that they find it offensive and rude. The fact is that someone at some point offended them or hurt them with those words. Someone they have already forgiven, but they have not forgiven the words. That's why they do not like those words but do not remember why not. They have forgiven the person but not the words, we all have those words that just burn in us. Words are alive and can burn deep.

We can stop the words, block them, and not let them hurt us, but that will only help temporarily.

It does not help if we do not forgive the person who says it, including their words, it will just create a different hold on our lives. The ripple effect of unforgiveness of negative words will reverberate into our spiritual growth and life, and because of someone else's wrong word choices, we will get stuck if we do not forgive.

Matthew 6:12

And forgive us our debts, as we also have forgiven our debtors.

Forgiveness is a must, not an option! Forgiveness is so important for us to be able to move on and

Words Matter

needs to happen before it's too late and do more damage. Even though God gives us a period of grace to forgive, because he knows what we need it and how long we need. It is still very important to let forgiveness into your heart, and the sooner the better. Time is not always on our side when it comes to unforgiveness.

It will be harder to forgive and forget the words that hurt us if those words live in our hearts and minds longer. When someone's words hurt, give them to God immediately and when you realise and remember words from your past, that burn inside you, give them to God and forgive.

We need to forgive 70 x 7 times, without limits. What is important to remember here is that most people speak out of ignorance when they throw negative words at us. They don't realise what they are doing and saying. Remembering this can make it easier and help to forgive them.

It's of course better if we can tell each other right away that what you just said was not right or acceptable, and sort the problem out just there and then. Then forgiveness can happen right there and then.

You will be surprised how many times you will hear in such a case, "It was just a joke." This of course, is just an excuse, and whether it is easy or not, to confront them and forgive them when they deny it or not. We still must forgive to make sure those words don't start burning in our hearts.

Words Matter
Luke 23:34
And Jesus said, "Father, forgive them, for they know not what they do." And they cast lots to divide His garments.

Just pretending nothing happened is not forgiving. You can't just put it away in a dark closet, forget it is there and move on with your life as if no one said or did something bad to you and didn't hurt you. You have to deal with it.

At some point, that closet is going to pop open, and all the bad things that people have said to you over time are going to tumble out.

Every time you do not forgive it starts to build up and will become too much to handle, you have to forgive! People's bad words can do a lot of damage to your future, without you realising it.

In our quest to be more like Jesus, it's important not to let all these words that the world burns us with change or damage our soul and our identity in Christ.

It is important to keep in mind how necessary forgiveness is for the words that come to harm, steal, and destroy, and to give that forgiveness to the people who spoke those words over our lives.

Whether it is words that people said to us a long, long time ago or just today. We must send them out of our lives and forgive them. Just like Jesus did when He died for us on the cross. Remember saying the words "I forgive you" doesn't mean you

Words Matter

did. You need to deal with it; it should come from the heart and soul, or else it is just empty words.

John 10:10

The thief comes only to steal, kill and destroy. I came that they may have life and have it abundantly.

"Lord, I forgive .... now, not only for his actions but for his words, I forgive the words and forget that it was spoken over me. In the name of Jesus Christ of Nazareth. Let the seeds that were just planted die. I will never remember what ….. was said to me. Amen"

Be specific when you pray, use the name of the person and the words that hurt you. Make sure that you completely surrender it to GOD.

What are the key takeaways from this chapter?

1. Words and unforgiveness.
2. It's one thing to forgive the person who spoke the words, but another to forgive the words.
3. The quicker we forgive, the better.
4. People don't realise their words are hurting you.
5. Make yourself heard.
6. Ignoring it is not forgiving.
7. Forgiveness for new and old words is so very important.
8. To be more like Jesus, we must forgive. As He did for us on the cross

Hebrews 10:26
For if we go on sinning
Deliberately
after receiving the knowledge of the

truth,

there no longer remains a sacrifice for

sins.

Chapter 23
Know the truth
John 8:32
Then you will know the truth and the Truth will set you free."

The knowledge of what our words can do to other people is a responsibility. One that we can no longer hide from, a responsibility that we must act on! It is our responsibility to think before we speak.

It is indeed something we have always known in our hearts and souls, that it is wrong when we say something bad, but we just don't think about it, while we are doing it. Maybe thought "Oh, the smaller words here and there don't matter." "No one takes the small bad things we say incorrectly, here and there, seriously anyway." If I slip up now and then and say something wrong to someone or about someone, it's not such a big deal.

But it's a big deal. A small bad word at the wrong time can be a final tear in an already fragile heart. There is no such thing as a small sin and a big sin. A sin is a sin. In the same way, there is neither a minor negative word nor a major negative word; wrong is wrong.

James 2:10

For whoever keeps the whole law but fails in one point has become guilty of all of it.

Now that you know the truth about what negative words can do to someone's soul, and how important words are, do you even dare speak one harmful word to someone?

Can you willingly and knowingly hurt someone with your words, knowing the consequences are big? Knowing you are planting seeds of insecurities that can do harm now and in the future?

From the moment you know the truth, you cannot deny it, and you are responsible for what you know and say. Using the wrong words when you know what you said or, are going to say is going to hurt someone is irresponsible.

Even if you just think there is a small chance it could hurt a person. It is your responsibility not to say it, or if you realised too late that your words were insensitive, fix it. Don't just pretend it didn't happen or pretend it's a joke.

If the thought occurs to you that the words you want to say, or have said to someone, may be wrong, you

Words Matter

already know it is wrong. That's the Holy Spirit warning you, and if you still let it happen, you are knowingly harming someone.

Knowing the truth is dangerous, because now that you know the truth, you cannot hide behind ignorance anymore. Now that you know the truth, you can no longer hide behind the words "I didn't realise or know what my words did or meant". Now that you know the truth, you have to live it! And knowing the truth and living the truth are two different things!

James 4:17

So, whoever knows the right thing to do and fails to do it, for him it is a sin.

What are the key takeaways from this chapter?

1. Know the truth.
2. The knowledge of what words can do carries responsibility.
3. Do you realise how harmful your negative words are?
4. here are no degrees of comparison when it comes to bad words.
5. Can you knowingly plant bad seeds?
6. You now know the truth.
7. Pro 24:12 If you say, "Behold, we did not know this," does not he who weighs the heart perceive it? Does not he who keeps watch over your soul know it, and will he not repay man according to his work?

JAMES 3:5-6

So also, the tongue is a small member, yet it boasts of great things. How great a forest is set ablaze by such a small

FIRE!

6 And the tongue is a fire, a world of unrighteousness. The tongue is set among our members, staining the

Whole Body,

setting on fire the entire course of life and set on fire by hell.

Words Matter

Chapter 24
Conclusion
Isaiah 51:10

Was it not you who dried up the sea, the waters? of the great deep, who made the depths of the sea? a way for the redeemed to pass over?

Just as God opened a way for His people through the sea, so He opens a way for us through the stormy sea of our life.

All we must do is set our feet in the water and put our trust in God, and He will keep our feet dry on the way forward.

He covers us in His shield and protects us from the stormy winds around us. He keeps us safe from the fiery tongues of the world. He protects

Words Matter

us and keeps us unstained from the scars of the fires and flames that the world throws at us.

James 3:5
So also, the tongue is a small member, yet it boasts. of great things. How great a forest is set ablaze by such a small fire!

Let go and let God have control of your life.
All we must do is keep trusting in God. Keep believing in our saviour! Keep having Faith in His love for us! He will keep the path open before us, and the flaming words of the fiery tongues of the world will not touch us.

For we are safely in His hands, protected against the stormy sea and the flames of the world.

The Word came to give us life. Life in abundance. Let your words do the same for the children of God.

Ephesians 6:16
In all circumstances take up the shield of faith, with which you can extinguish all the flaming darts of the evil one. 17 and take the helmet of salvation, and the sword of the Spirit, which is the word of God,

Joshua 3:17
Now the priests bearing the ark of the covenant. of the LORD stood firmly on dry ground in the midst of the Jordan, and all Israel was passing over on dry ground until all the nation finished passing. over the Jordan.

Words Matter

What are the key takeaways from this chapter?

1. Conclusion.
2. Trust in God.
3. God will keep us safe from the fiery tongues of the world.
4. Let go and give it to God.
5. Keep Believing in our saviour.
6. Let your words do the same for God's children.

Notes

Words Matter

Verse Index
Old Testament
Genesis
- Gen 2:18 Then the LORD God said, "It is not good that the man should be alone; I will make him a helper fit for him."
- Gen 3:16 ASV Unto the woman he said, I will greatly multiply thy pain and thy conception; in pain, thou shalt bring forth children; and thy desire shall be to thy husband, and he shall rule over thee.
- Gen 12:1-4 Now the LORD said to Abram, "Go from your country and your kindred and your father's house to the land that I will show you.2 And I will make of you a great nation, and I will bless you and make your name great so that you will be a blessing. 3 I will bless those who bless you, and him who dishonours you I will curse, and in you all the families of the earth shall be blessed."4 So Abram went, as the LORD had told him, and Lot went with him. Abram was seventy-five years old when he departed from Haran.
- Gen 22:2-3 He said, "Take your son, your only son Isaac, whom you love, and go to the land of Moriah, and offer him there as a burnt offering on one of the mountains of which I shall tell you."3 So Abraham rose early in the morning, saddled his donkey, and took two of

his young men with him, and his son Isaac. And he cut the wood for the burnt offering and arose and went to the place of which God had told him.

Exodus

- Exo 23:1 "You shall not spread a false report. You shall not join hands with a wicked man to be a malicious witness.

Deuteronomy

- Deu 4:9 "Only take care, and keep your soul diligently, lest you forget the things that your eyes have seen, and lest they depart from your heart all the days of your life. Make them known to your children and your children's children—
- Deu 6:6-7 And these words that I command you today shall be on your heart.7 You shall teach them diligently to your children, and shall talk of them when you sit in your house, and when you walk by the way, and when you lie down, and when you rise
- Deu 31:6 Be strong and courageous. Do not fear or be in dread of them, for it is the LORD your God who goes with you. He will not leave you or forsake you."

Joshua

- Jos 3:17 Now the priests bearing the ark of the covenant of the LORD stood firmly on dry ground in the midst of the Jordan, and all

Words Matter

Israel was passing over on dry ground until all the nation finished passing over the Jordan.
- Jos 6:16 And at the seventh time, when the priests had blown the trumpets, Joshua said to the people, "Shout, for the LORD has given you the city.

1 and 2 Samuel
- **1Sa 2:1** And Hannah prayed and said, "My heart exults in the LORD; my horn is exalted in the LORD. My mouth derides my enemies because I rejoice in your salvation.
- **2Sa 22:1** And David spoke to the LORD the words of this song on the day when the LORD delivered him from the hand of all his enemies, and from the hand of Saul.

JOB
- Job 4:4 Your words have upheld him who was stumbling, and you have made firm the feeble knees.

Psalm
- Psa 9:1-2 To the choirmaster: according to Muth-labben. A Psalm of David. I will give thanks to the LORD with my whole heart; I will recount all of your wonderful deeds. 2 I will be glad and exult in you; I will sing praise to your name, O Most High.
- Psa 15:4 A Psalm of David. O LORD, who shall sojourn in your tent? Who shall dwell on your holy hill? 2 He who walks blamelessly and does what is right and speaks truth in his

Words Matter

heart; 3 Who does not slander with his tongue and does no evil to his neighbour, nor takes up a reproach against his friend; 4 in whose eyes a vile person is despised, but who honours those who fear the LORD; who swears to his own hurt and does not change.

- Psa 23:4-5 Even though I walk through the valley of the shadow of death, I will fear no evil, for you are with me; your rod and your staff, they comfort me. 5 You prepare a table before me in the presence of my enemies; you anoint my head with oil; my cup overflows.
- Psa 62:2 He alone is my rock and my salvation, my fortress; I shall not be greatly shaken.
- Psa 96V1-3 Oh sing to the LORD a new song; sing to the LORD, all the earth! 2 Sing to the LORD, bless his name; tell of his salvation from day to day. 3 Declare his glory among the nations, his marvelous works among all the peoples!
- Psa 100:1-2 A Psalm for giving thanks Make a joyful noise to the LORD all the earth! 2 Serve the LORD with gladness! Come into his presence with singing!
- Psa 119:145-147 Qoph With my whole heart I cry; answer me, O LORD! I will keep your statutes.146 I call to you; save me, that I may observe your testimonies.147 I rise before dawn and cry for help; I hope in your words.

Words Matter

- Psa 139 v 4 Even before a word is on my tongue, behold, O LORD, you know it altogether.
- Psa 141:2-4 Let my prayer be counted as incense before you, and the lifting up of my hands as the evening sacrifice! 3 Set a guard, O LORD, over my mouth; keep watch over the door of my lips! 4 Do not let my heart incline to any evil, to busy myself with wicked deeds in company with men who work iniquity and let me not eat of their delicacies!

<u>Proverbs</u>
- Pro 4:23-24 Keep your heart with all vigilance, for from it flow the springs of life. 24 Put away from you crooked speech and put devious talk far from you.
- Pro 10:18-21 The one who conceals hatred has lying lips, and whoever utters slander is a fool. 19 When words are many, transgression is not lacking, but whoever restrains his lips is prudent. 20 The tongue of the righteous is choice silver; the heart of the wicked is of little worth. 21 The lips of the righteous feed many, but fools die for lack of sense.
- Pro 11:1 A false balance is an abomination to the LORD, but a just weight is his delight.
- Pro 11:9 With his mouth the godless man would destroy his neighbour, but by knowledge, the righteous are delivered.

Words Matter

- Pro 12:22 Lying lips are an abomination to the LORD, but those who act faithfully are his delight.
- Pro 12:25 Anxiety in a man's heart weighs him down, but a good word makes him glad.
- Pro 14:3 By the mouth of a fool comes a rod for his back, but the lips of the wise will preserve them.
- Pro 15:1 -4 A soft answer turns away wrath, but a harsh word stirs up anger. 2 The tongue of the wise commends knowledge, but the mouths of fools pour out folly. 3 The eyes of the LORD are in every place, keeping watch on the evil and the good. 4 A gentle tongue is a tree of life, but perverseness in it breaks the spirit.
- Pro 15:23 To make an apt answer is a joy to a man, and a word in season, how good it is!
- Pro 16:24 Gracious words are like a honeycomb, sweetness to the soul and health to the body
- Pro 17:27-28 Whoever restrains his words has knowledge, and he who has a cool spirit is a man of understanding. 28 Even a fool who keeps silent is considered wise; when he closes his lips, he is deemed intelligent.
- Pro 18:4 The words of a man's mouth are deep waters; the fountain of wisdom is a bubbling brook

Words Matter
- Pro 18:21 Death and life are in the power of the tongue, and those who love it will eat its fruits.
- Pro 22:6 Train up a child in the way he should go; even when he is old, he will not depart from it.
- Pro 26:18-19 Like a madman who throws firebrands, arrows, and death 19 is the man who deceives his neighbour and says, "I am only joking!"
- Pro 27:17 Iron sharpens iron, and one man sharpens another.
- Pro 29:20 Do you see a man who is hasty in his words? There is more hope for a fool than for him.
- Pro 31:10-12 An excellent wife who can find? She is far more precious than jewels.11 The heart of her husband trusts in her, and he will have no lack of gain.12 She does him good, and not harm, all the days of her life.
- Pro 31:26 She opens her mouth with wisdom, and the teaching of kindness is on her tongue.

Ecclesiastes
- Ecc 3:7 a time to tear, and a time to sew; a time to keep silence, and a time to speak.
- Ecc 4:6 Better is a handful of quietness than two hands full of toil and a striving after wind.
- Ecc 5:2 Be not rash with your mouth, nor let your heart be hasty to utter a word before

Words Matter

God, for God is in heaven and you are on earth. Therefore let your words be few.
- Ecc 7:1 A good name is better than precious ointment, and the day of death than the day of birth.

<u>Isaiah</u>
- Isa 6:8-10 And I heard the voice of the Lord saying, "Whom shall I send, and who will go for us?" Then I said, "Here I am! Send me." 9 And he said, "Go, and say to this people: "'Keep on hearing, but do not understand; keep on seeing, but do not perceive.' 10 Make the heart of this people dull, and their ears heavy, and blind their eyes; lest they see with their eyes, and hear with their ears, and understand with their hearts, and turn and be healed."
- Isa 43:1 But now thus says the LORD, he who created you, O Jacob, he who formed you, O Israel: "Fear not, for I have redeemed you; I have called you by name, you are mine.
- Isa 51:10 Was it not you who dried up the sea, the waters of the great deep, who made the depths of the sea a way for the redeemed to pass over?
- Isa 55:8-10 For my thoughts are not your thoughts, neither are your ways my ways, declares the LORD. 9 For as the heavens are higher than the earth, so are my ways higher than your ways and my thoughts than your

Words Matter

thoughts. 10 "For as the rain and the snow come down from heaven and do not return there but water the earth, making it bring forth and sprout, giving seed to the sower and bread to the eater,

Jeremiah
- Jer 9:8 Their tongue is a deadly arrow; it speaks deceitfully; with his mouth, each speaks peace to his neighbour, but in his heart, he plans an ambush for him.

Zechariah
- Zec 8:16 These are the things that you shall do: Speak the truth to one another; render in your gates judgments that are true and make for peace.

New Testament
Matthew
- Mat 4:19 And he said to them, "Follow me, and I will make you fishers of men."
- Mat 6:12 and forgive us our debts, as we also have forgiven our debtors.
- Mat 9:37-38 Then he said to his disciples, "The harvest is plentiful, but the laborers are few; 38, therefore, pray earnestly to the Lord of the harvest to send out laborers into his harvest."
- Mat 10:8 Heal the sick, raise the dead, cleanse lepers, cast out demons. You received without paying; give without pay.

Words Matter

- Mat 11:28-30 Come to me, all who labor and are heavy laden, and I will give you rest. 29 Take my yoke upon you, and learn from me, for I am gentle and lowly in heart, and you will find rest for your souls. 30 For my yoke is easy, and my burden is light."
- Mat 12:36-37 I tell you, on the day of judgment people will give account for every careless word they speak, 37for by your words you will be justified, and by your words, you will be condemned."
- Mat 15:7-8 You hypocrites! Well did Isaiah prophesy of you, when he said: 8 "This people honours me with their lips, but their heart is far from me;
- Mat 18:15-17 "If your brother sins against you, go and tell him his fault, between you and him alone. If he listens to you, you have gained your brother. 16 But if he does not listen, take one or two others along with you, that every charge may be established by the evidence of two or three witnesses. 17 If he refuses to listen to them, tell it to the church. And if he refuses to listen even to the church, let him be to you as a Gentile and a tax collector.
- Mat 18:21-22 Then Peter came up and said to him, "Lord, how often will my brother sin against me, and I forgive him? As many as seven times?" 22 Jesus said to him, "I do not

Words Matter

say to you seven times, but seventy-seven times.
- Mat 21:21 And Jesus answered them, "Truly, I say to you, if you have faith and do not doubt, you will not only do what has been done to the fig tree, but even if you say to this mountain, 'Be taken up and thrown into the sea,' it will happen.
- Mat 22:36-39 "Teacher, which is the great commandment in the Law?" 37 And he said to him, "You shall love the Lord your God with all your heart and with all your soul and with all your mind. 38 This is the great and first commandment. 39 And a second is like it: You shall love your neighbour as yourself.
- Mat 25:35-40 For I was hungry, and you gave me food, I was thirsty and you gave me drink, I was a stranger and you welcomed me, 36 I was naked, and you clothed me, I was sick and you visited me, I was in prison and you came to me.' 37 Then the righteous will answer him, saying, 'Lord, when did we see you hungry and feed you, or thirsty and give you drink? 38 And when did we see you a stranger and welcome you, or naked and clothe you? 39 And when did we see you sick or in prison and visit you?' 40 And the King will answer them, 'Truly, I say to you, as you did it to one of the least of these my brothers, you did it to me.'

Words Matter

Mark

- Mar 10:45 For even the Son of Man came not to be served but to serve, and to give his life as a ransom for many."
- Mar 2:29-31 Jesus answered, "The most important is, 'Hear, O Israel: The Lord our God, the Lord is one. 30 And you shall love the Lord your God with all your heart and with all your soul and with all your mind and with all your strength.' 31 The second is this: 'You shall love your neighbour as yourself.' There is no other commandment greater than these."
- Mar 16:17-18 And these signs will accompany those who believe in my name they will cast out demons; they will speak in new tongues; 18 they will pick up serpents with their hands; and if they drink any deadly poison, it will not hurt them; they will lay their hands on the sick, and they will recover."

Luke

- Luk 1:46-48 And Mary said, "My soul magnifies the Lord, 47 and my spirit rejoices in God my Savior, 48 for he has looked on the humble estate of his servant. For behold, from now on all generations will call me blessed.
- Luk 1:67-68 And his father Zechariah was filled with the Holy Spirit and prophesied,

Words Matter

saying, 68 "Blessed be the Lord God of Israel, for he has visited and redeemed his people.
- Luk 6:45-48 The good person out of the good treasure of his heart produces good, and the evil person out of his evil treasure produces evil, for out of the abundance of the heart his mouth speaks. 46 "Why do you call me 'Lord, Lord,' and not do what I tell you? 47 Everyone who comes to me and hears my words and does them, I will show you what he is like 48 he is like a man building a house, who dug deep and laid the foundation on the rock. And when a flood arose, the stream broke against that house and could not shake it, because it had been well built.
- Luk 8:17 For nothing is hidden that will not be made manifest, nor is anything secret that will not be known and come to light.
- Luk 12:2-3 Nothing is covered up that will not be revealed or hidden that will not be known. 3 Therefore whatever you have said in the dark shall be heard in the light, and what you have whispered in private rooms shall be proclaimed on the housetops.
- Luk 16:10 "One who is faithful in a very little is also faithful in much, and one who is dishonest in a very little is also dishonest in much.
- Luk 21:33 Heaven and earth will pass away,

Words Matter

but my words will not pass away.
- Luk 23:34 And Jesus said, "Father, forgive them, for they know not what they do." And they cast lots to divide his garments.

<u>John</u>
- Joh 1:1-5 In the beginning was the Word, and the Word was with God, and the Word was God. 2 He was in the beginning with God. 3 All things were made through him, and without him was not anything made that was made. 4 In him was life, and the life was the light of men. 5 The light shines in the darkness, and the darkness has not overcome it.
- Joh 1:12-13 But to all who did receive him, who believed in his name, he gave the right to become children of God, 13 who were born, not of blood nor of the will of the flesh nor of the will of man, but of God.
- Joh 1:14 And the Word became flesh and dwelt among us, and we have seen his glory, glory as of the only Son from the Father, full of grace and truth.
- Joh 3:16 "For God so loved the world, that he gave his only Son, that whoever believes in him should not perish but have eternal life.
- Joh 7:38 Whoever believes in me, as the Scripture has said, 'Out of his heart will flow rivers of living water.'"

Words Matter

- Joh 8:32 and you will know the truth, and the truth will set you free."
- Joh 10:10 The thief comes only to steal and kill and destroy. I came that they may have life and have it abundantly.
- John 12:46-47 I have come into the world as light so that whoever believes in me may not remain in darkness. 47 If anyone hears my words and does not keep them, I do not judge him; for I did not come to judge the world but to save the world.
- Joh 13:12-15 When he had washed their feet and put on his outer garments and resumed his place, he said to them, "Do you understand what I have done to you? 13 You call me Teacher and Lord, and you are right, for so I am.14 If I then, your Lord and Teacher, have washed your feet, you also ought to wash one another's feet. 15 For I have given you an example, that you also should do just as I have done to you.
- Joh 14:12-13 "Truly, truly, I say to you, whoever believes in me will also do the works that I do; and greater works than these will he do, because I am going to the Father.13 Whatever you ask in my name, this I will do, that the Father may be glorified in the Son. 14 If you ask me anything in my name, I will do it.
- Joh 14:26-27 But the Helper, the Holy Spirit,

whom the Father will send in my name, he will teach you all things and bring to your remembrance all that I have said to you. 27 Peace I leave with you; my peace I give to you. Not as the world gives do I give to you. Let not your hearts be troubled, neither let them be afraid.

- Joh 15:7 If you abide in me, and my words abide in you, ask whatever you wish, and it will be done for you.
- Joh 15:13-15 Greater love has no one than this, that someone lay down his life for his friends. 14 You are my friends if you do what I command you. 15 No longer do I call you servants, for the servant does not know what his master is doing; but I have called you friends, for all that I have heard from my Father I have made known to you.

Acts

- Act 1:5 for John baptized with water, but you will be baptized with the Holy Spirit not many days from now."
- Act 1:8 But you will receive power when the Holy Spirit has come upon you, and you will be my witnesses in Jerusalem and in all Judea and Samaria, and to the end of the earth."
- Act 13:47 For so the Lord has commanded us, saying, "'I have made you a light for the

Words Matter

Gentiles, that you may bring salvation to the ends of the earth.'"

Romans
- Rom 12:2 Do not be conformed to this world, but be transformed by the renewal of your mind, that by testing you may discern what is the will of God, what is good and acceptable and perfect.
- Rom 12:19 Beloved, never avenge yourselves, but leave it to the wrath of God, for it is written, "Vengeance is mine, I will repay, says the Lord."

1 Corinthians
- 1Co 12:8 For to one is given through the Spirit the utterance of wisdom, and to another the utterance of knowledge according to the same Spirit.
- 1Co 1:5-7 that in every way you were enriched in him in all speech and all knowledge 6 even as the testimony about Christ was confirmed among you 7 so that you are not lacking in any gift, as you wait for the revealing of our Lord Jesus Christ,
- 1Co 13:1 If I speak in the tongues of men and of angels, but have not love, I am a noisy gong or a clanging cymbal.
- 1Co 13:4-5 Love is patient and kind; love does not envy or boast; it is not arrogant. 5 or rude. It does not insist on its own way; it is not irritable or resentful.

Words Matter

- 1Co 13:9-10 For we know in part, and we prophesy in part. 10 but when the perfect comes, the partial will pass away.
- 1Co 13:13 So now faith, hope, and love abide, these three; but the greatest of these is love.

2 Corinthians
- 2Co 1:20-22 For all the promises of God find their Yes in him. That is why it is through him that we utter our Amen to God for his glory. 21 And it is God who establishes us with you in Christ and has anointed us, 22 and who has also put his seal on us and given us his Spirit in our hearts as a guarantee.

Galatians
- Gal 3:26-29 for in Christ Jesus you are all sons of God, through faith. 27 For as many of you as were baptized into Christ have put on Christ. 28 There is neither Jew nor Greek, there is neither slave nor free, there is no male and female, for you are all one in Christ Jesus. 29 And if you are Christ's, then you are Abraham's offspring, heirs according to promise.
- Gal 4:5-7 to redeem those who were under the law, so that we might receive adoption as sons. 6 And because you are sons, God has sent the Spirit of his Son into our hearts, crying, "Abba! Father!" 7 So you are no longer a slave, but a son, and if a son, then an heir through God.

Words Matter
- Gal 6:6-8 Let the one who is taught the word share all good things with the one who teaches. 7 Do not be deceived: God is not mocked, for whatever one sows, that will he also reap. 8 For he that soweth to his flesh shall of the flesh reap corruption; but he that soweth to the Spirit shall of the Spirit reap life everlasting.

Ephesians
- Eph 2:10 For we are his workmanship, created in Christ Jesus for good works, which God prepared beforehand, that we should walk in them.
- Eph 4:25 Therefore having put away falsehood let each one of you speak the truth with his neighbour, for we are members one of another.
- Eph 4:29 Let no corrupting talk come out of your mouths, but only such as is good for building up, as fits the occasion, that it may give grace to those who hear.
- Eph 5:4 Let there be no filthiness nor foolish talk nor crude joking, which are out of place, but instead, let there be thanksgiving.
- Eph 5:18-20 And do not get drunk with wine, for that is debauchery, but be filled with the Spirit, 19 addressing one another in psalms and hymns and spiritual songs, singing and making melody to the Lord with your heart, 20 giving thanks always and for

everything to God the Father in the name of our Lord Jesus Christ,

- Eph 6:4 Fathers, do not provoke your children to anger but bring them up in the discipline and instruction of the Lord.
- Eph 6:13-16. Therefore, take up the whole Armor of God, that you may be able to withstand in the evil day, and having done all, to stand firm. 14 Stand therefore, having fastened on the belt of truth, and having put on the breastplate of righteousness, 15 and, as shoes for your feet, having put on the readiness given by the gospel of peace. 16 In all circumstances take up the shield of faith, with which you can extinguish all the flaming darts of the evil one.

Philippians

- Phi 4:6-7 do not be anxious about anything, but in everything by prayer and supplication with thanksgiving let your requests be made known to God. 7 And the peace of God, which surpasses all understanding, will guard your hearts and your minds in Christ Jesus.

Colossians

- Col 3:8 But now you must put them all away: anger, wrath, malice, slander, and obscene talk from your mouth.
- Col 3:17 And whatever you do, in word or deed, do everything in the name of the Lord Jesus, giving thanks to God the Father

Words Matter

through him.
- Col 4:5-6 Walk in wisdom toward outsiders, making the best use of the time. **6** Let your speech always be gracious, seasoned with salt, so that you may know how you ought to answer each person.

<u>1 Thessalonians</u>
- 1Th 5:11 Therefore encourage one another and build one another up, just as you are doing.

<u>2 Timothy</u>
- 2Ti 1:7 for God gave us a spirit not of fear but of power and love and self-control.

<u>Hebrews</u>
- Heb 8:12 For I will be merciful toward their iniquities, and I will remember their sins no more."
- Heb 10:26 For if we go on sinning deliberately after receiving the knowledge of the truth, there no longer remains a sacrifice for sins,
- Heb 11:1-3 Now faith is the assurance of things hoped for, the conviction of things not seen. 2 For by it the people of old received their commendation. 3 By faith we understand that the universe was created by the word of God, so that what is seen was not made out of things that are visible.

Words Matter

- Heb 13:2 Do not neglect to show hospitality to strangers, for thereby some have entertained angels unawares.
- Heb 13:8 Jesus Christ is the same yesterday and today and forever.

James

- Jas 1:2-4 Count it all joy, my brothers, when you meet trials of various kinds, 3 for you know that the testing of your faith produces steadfastness. 4 And let steadfastness have its full effect, that you may be perfect and complete, lacking in nothing.
- Jas 1:13-14 Let no one say when he is tempted, "I am being tempted by God," for God cannot be tempted with evil, and he himself tempts no one. 14 But each person is tempted when he is lured and enticed by his own desire.
- Jas 1: 19-20 Know this my beloved brothers let every person be quick to hear, slow to speak, slow to anger; 20 for the anger of man does not produce the righteousness of God.
- Jas 1:26 If anyone thinks he is religious and does not bridle his tongue but deceives his heart, this person's religion is worthless.
- Jas 2:10 For whoever keeps the whole law but fails in one point has become guilty of all of it.
- Jas 3: 2-12 For we all stumble in many ways. And if anyone does not stumble in what he

Words Matter

says, he is a perfect man, able also to bridle his whole body. 3 If we put bits into the mouths of horses so that they obey us, we guide their whole bodies as well. 4 Look at the ships also: though they are so large and are driven by strong winds, they are guided by a very small rudder wherever the will of the pilot directs. 5 So also the tongue is a small member, yet it boasts of great things. How great a forest is set ablaze by such a small fire! 6 And the tongue is a fire, a world of unrighteousness. The tongue is set among our members, staining the whole body, setting on fire the entire course of life, and set on fire by hell. 7 For every kind of beast and bird, of reptile and sea creature, can be tamed and has been tamed by mankind, 8 but no human being can tame the tongue. It is a restless evil, full of deadly poison. 9 With it we bless our Lord and Father, and with it, we curse people who are made in the likeness of God. 10 From the same mouth come blessing and cursing. My brothers, these things ought not to be so. 11 Does a spring pour forth from the same opening both fresh and saltwater?

- Jas 4:11-12 Do not speak evil against one another, brothers. The one who speaks against a brother or judges his brother, speaks evil against the law and judges the

law. But if you judge the law, you are not a doer of the law but a judge. 12 There is only one lawgiver and judge, he who is able to save and to destroy. But who are you to judge your neighbour
- Jas 4:17 CSB So it is sin to know the good and yet not do it.

1Peter

- 1Pe 2:6-8 For it stands in Scripture: "Behold, I am laying in Zion a stone, a cornerstone chosen and precious, and whoever believes in him will not be put to shame." 7 So the honour is for you who believe, but for those who do not believe, "The stone that the builders rejected has become the cornerstone," 8 and "A stone of stumbling, and a rock of offense." They stumble because they disobey the word, as they were destined to do.
- 1 Pe 3:9-12 Do not repay evil for evil or reviling for reviling, but on the contrary, bless, for to this you were called, that you may obtain a blessing. 10 For "Whoever desires to love life and see good days, let him keep his tongue from evil and his lips from speaking deceit; 11 let him turn away from evil and do good; let him seek peace and pursue it. 12 For the eyes of the Lord are on the righteous, and his ears are open to their prayer. But the face of the Lord is against those who do evil."

Words Matter

- 1 Pe 4:9-11 Show hospitality to one another without grumbling. 10 As each has received a gift, use it to serve one another, as good stewards of God's varied grace.

1John
- 1Jn 3:18 NIV Dear children, let us not love with words or speech. But with actions and in truth.
- 1Jn 5:7-8 KVJ For there are three that bear record in heaven, the Father, the Word, and the Holy Ghost: and these three are one. 8 And there are three that bear witness in earth, the Spirit, and the water, and the blood: and these three agree in one.

www.ingramcontent.com/pod-product-compliance
Lightning Source LLC
Chambersburg PA
CBHW060316050426
42449CB00011B/2505